Control Your Processes...Control Your Profits

Process-focused Approaches to Running

Businesses Profitably

Cameron Howe P.Eng. MBA

ISBN-10: 1489586547
ISBN-13: 9781489586544

DEDICATION

Special thanks to my family for your endless support and patience while I remained tethered to my laptop for the last two years. Thanks to my parents for introducing me to the world of entrepreneurship. Thanks to Allanah, Karen, Denise and Suzie for their professional input. Thanks to the Imperial College Business School and the University of Toronto, Faculty of Applied Science & Engineering for the rewarding, enlightening and sometimes painful journey.

To the Entrepreneur:

Hold on tightly to your entrepreneurial dreams; careful never to acquiesce to the whims or the surreptitious devices of others. Despite the hardships that surely will come and feel like the darkest of days, let reason guide you and let passion carry you through to better times. The road that you have chosen will yield riches that transcend any monetary rewards. It will provide you with the greatest gift of all – true independence.

Cameron D. Howe

Introduction

Over the years, I have read some excellent and enlightening business books written by authors such as Drucker, McGrath, White and Bagley. Great stuff, and highly recommended. Then there are the *other* types of books that I whole-heartedly *do not* recommend. These books are part of the reason why I wrote this book and with regard to them, I need to say that I am not happy; not happy at all. If you have ever read any of these books, then you will have noticed how these authors seem to follow a similar two-step formula. First, they present "ground-breaking" advice that is, in fact, trivial and obvious. Then, if that isn't bad enough, the premise of their book is usually based on one unique point to which the author clings relentlessly. You first notice when you are reading one of these books when each and every story ends up having exactly the same moral. And here is the predominant feeling that you will experience when reading one of these books: *disbelief.* Utter disbelief, as you realize that you were not just duped out of your money, you also had hopes of learning something truly new and useful dashed. I've been there too; more than once.

Another thing that irks me about certain types of books is the relentless self-promotion (insert *"Limited seating seminar at the Holiday Inn!!!!"* here) while scarcely addressing the needs of the most important person of all: **_YOU_**, the Customer! Seriously, you were kind enough to hand over your hard earned cash for the book, so the last thing that you deserve is to be shamelessly upsold. *"No good deed goes unpunished"* – is an apt reference to these authors taking your money for their wares.

While I'm on my rant, I should mention another problem that I have with many business books: *sensationalism and hyperbole*. These are used nefariously by authors who tell would-be entrepreneurs that starting a business is a dead easy road to riches. Well, in my humble opinion: NOT TRUE!

Now, here are the cold, hard facts, hyperbole aside. Starting a business is fraught with unknowns and unknowables and no author's "How To" book or seminar that can assure your passage through these potentially stormy seas. The best that any author can *promise* is that they have provided you with the tools that will help to increase your odds of success. That's right, *odds* of success. And this is only half the battle because it's not just about starting the business. It's about starting a *profitable* one; one that has optimized all of its processes. This is certainly more in line with my approach. I strongly believe that knowledge *is* power and ignorance is certainly not bliss; it's actually more like a death knell.

In this book I am going to give you honest and pragmatic advice based on my experience and education; and most importantly, I am telling you upfront that trying to start a business is a risky undertaking because, *there are no guarantees*. Speaking of risk, you should know that risk is _not_ your enemy. Risk is simply a fundamental part of the game and it just needs to be managed, not feared. Risk keeps you vigilant and forces you to think about every decision that you make with a long-term cause and effect perspective.

Despite their reputation as risk takers and mavericks, entrepreneurs are typically risk-averse individuals who mitigate and manage risk through the acquisition of knowledge and through careful preparation. For this reason, entrepreneurs should more accurately be described as risk managers _not_ risk takers. Any gamblers in the crowd should avoid entrepreneurial endeavors like the plague – you _will_ lose this gamble. Risk managers are welcomed.

My objective in writing this book was quite clear. I decided to write what I believe is a most useful and _practical_ book that provides a prescriptive approach to starting a profitable business or more effectively running one that is already established. The fundamental argument or thesis that is supported is the necessity to control processes with steely-eyed determination if one is to achieve and sustain maximal profitability. Why is this? Because business and manufacturing processes aggregate like a long continuous chain; _and I'm sure that the concept of the weakest link and its implications are universally understood._

Have you ever had a conversation with a friend or colleague and at some point in the discussion something is said - sometimes only a single word - that illuminates the proverbial light bulb above your head? I see my *duty* to you and to your venture as being a personal facilitator that will help to get this light bulb lit. To that end, you will be peppered – no, actually you will be *inundated* - with concepts, anecdotes, ideas and examples. Best of all, this process will not be done in a drawn-out, repetitive manner and certainly not in the form of a cleverly scripted promotion piece to be used as an up-sale.

Before we delve into the book's core material, let's briefly explore the connection between processes and profits. So what processes are critical to maximizing profits? Let's examine a few examples:

- The process of finding a need or problem to solve

- Determining a viable solution to the problem

- Establishing a business case that justifies the solution

- Undertaking an micro/macroeconomic strategic analysis of the solution

- Quantifying and gathering the resources required to implement solution

- Executing the numerous interconnected and disparate

processes of establishing the business

- Managing resources during and after business establishment

- Refining newly established manufacturing/business processes to yield highest profits

- Implementing new processes based on market demand, social or technological changes

- Identifying new business opportunities directly related to the current product/service (such as vertical integration)

- Identifying new business opportunities not related to the current solution (diversification)

We will explore all of these processes as well as many others within the context of both business start-ups and improvements to going concerns. You paid for a book that will help you to start a profitable business or improve an existing one, and that is what you have received. Your good deed *will* be rewarded. Through experience and education I have learned the language of business start-up and process improvement; and I am here to share that with you.

CONTENTS

Chapter 1 – One Entrepreneur's Perspective

"The critical ingredient is getting off your butt and doing something. It's as simple as that. A lot of people have ideas, but there are few who decide to do something about them now. Not tomorrow. Not next week, but today. The true entrepreneur is a doer, not a dreamer."

Nolan Bushnell

I am pretty sure that I know what you are thinking: "just who is this Cameron Howe guy and what can I possibly gain from reading this *Control Your Processes...Control Your Profits* thing?" Well, the answer is that you will gain a substantial amount of knowledge about how to start and run a business profitably. All that you need to do is put in the effort and I assure you that you will learn an amazing amount about entrepreneurship, executing start-ups, business process improvement and business analysis. Before we delve into the core material, I strongly encourage you to read this chapter thoroughly as it will provide you with the "big picture" and an explanation of how my experiences ended up as a book that will provide you with significant help in your quest to start a profitable business or to improve the one that you already run. I assure you that it will be worth it.

So what about my actual small business experience? Well, you could say that I have *been there, done that*. I have enjoyed the successes and admittedly I have stepped in many proverbial bear traps along the way. The really good news for you is that you can benefit from my experiences by learning how to make the wins while at the same time, sparing your ankles from the ravages of those bear traps. Now, with that in mind, allow me to back up a bit to give you a brief historical perspective on my life as an entrepreneur.

As long as I can remember I have been fascinated with the entrepreneurial process; and it came really early. When I was eight years old, I was snooping around my parent's basement when I happened upon a dusty old box filled with many small tins of table wax. I asked my mother if I could have them. Naturally she probed further, asking me what I wanted to do with them. With a partially toothed grin, I responded: "I'm going to *sell* them!" Well, my mother was never one to stand in the way of progress, so she obliged. Next, my best friend and I proceeded to go from door to door in our neighborhood making *the pitch*. Responses from our "customers" were sharply divided and fell into two basic categories; from *"do your mothers know what we were doing?"* to *"fifty cents? That sounds fair; I'll take two - thanks boys!"* In the end, all of the waxes were sold and from that moment I was bitten by the entrepreneurial bug.

As a kid, the profit-making process utterly and completely fascinated me. To me, it was like creating something from nothing. This fascination was the driving force for my engagement in countless deals with other kids in my neighborhood. I would trade items that could not be easily sold for cash for other items that could be and then I would sell them…for CASH!! For example, when I was eleven, I remember trading a $7 radio for a telescope and then selling that telescope for $150. Believe me, that was a fortune for an eleven year old! To this day, I clearly remember the way that I clinched the sale. I situated the telescope in our living room and aimed it at a thermometer on the neighbor's house that was about *200 feet away*. When the gentleman (yes, I was sometimes selling to adults, which seemed a bit daunting) looked through the telescope he could see the thermometer *clearer than if he was standing two feet away from it*. All he said was "wow!…..seventy eight degrees". Next, he reached into his pocket and handed me the money; no bartering, no negotiations. He was thoroughly convinced.

From the ages of 13 to 15, I used to routinely pay $5-$10 for old bicycles, clean them up and then sell them for $40 to $50. I would also buy broken audio/video equipment with cosmetic or superficial problems - like a broken wire or drive belt - and then I would repair the equipment and sell it for a substantial profit. Many years later, I dealt with larger items such as motorcycles, cars and eventually houses....and best of all, this was fun!

Fast forward to my high school years when I turned my passion for music and sound systems into a part-time business by making and selling audio speakers. I designed the speaker cabinets, specified the hardware components, approached component manufacturers and bought parts in bulk to secure good prices. With the parts in hand, I did the carpentry/finishing and assembly and then used the local newspaper to market and sell the speakers. I have to admit, it wasn't easy to sell them. People were understandably dubious about committing to no-name speakers - my first lesson on the power of branding. However, when I could convince them to come to my house to listen to them *with their favorite music*; to lift them up and inspect the workmanship, more often than not,

I made the sale. In hindsight, though running the company was a tremendous amount of work, once again to me it was just fun. The entrepreneurial bug bit hard that time.

Fast forward fifteen years, when I became a full time entrepreneur. Once again, a hobby turned profession; and this time it was brewing and selling beer. For years, I had been perfecting my beer making skills and sharing the results with my friends. So, in addition to becoming THE most popular guy in the neighborhood, I got pretty good at making eclectic and unusual beers that couldn't be found anywhere – with the possible exception of deepest darkest Bavaria. After I graduated from university as a chemical engineer, I decided to combine everything that I knew about the art of beer making with my technical knowledge to investigate the start-up of a microbrewery. A few years later, after much planning and preparation, I co-founded the microbrewery with my mother (see how far you can come from table wax!) sister and brother-in-law.

To get the brewery started, I worked on the business plan day and night, consulted with bar owners, materials suppliers, lawyers, accountants, real estate people, brewers, skilled trades, liquor regulatory boards and bankers. I learned how to

TIG weld so that I could fabricate and maintain equipment. I learned basic accounting so that I could prepare rudimentary financial projections. I literally wore a dozen hats while building that company - as did my partners. In the end, we took a concept written on paper and transformed it into a multi-million dollar business. We became quite successful, dubbed the "City's Best New Beer" by a high profile magazine. We got significant press for our beers and our unique 9-pack in the U.S. and Canada and won the most prestigious awards that a brewery can win: a World Beer Cup®. It was the thrill of a lifetime and not one minute of the time that I dedicated to that project felt like "a job".

As time moved on and the business matured, my family and I got an excellent opportunity to sell our positions and exit the company. Having been through three major rounds of funding to expand the business, we decided that it was time to *receive* some big cheques for a change instead of writing them (for the upcoming fourth round of funding). So we decided to take that opportunity and we "cashed out" as they say. Note, later on in the book I discuss the importance and implications of having a well-defined exit strategy *from the beginning*.

So, with the company sold and with no immediate plans for

another start-up, I decided to do the unthinkable - from an entrepreneur's perspective anyway. I decided to venture back into the working world as *an employee* (yikes!!); *but temporarily*. Now, as a person interested in entrepreneurship, you might liken a return to employee status as a voluntary prison term. I however, did not see it that way. Corporations of all sizes present fantastic opportunities for entrepreneurs, or perhaps more accurately, intrapreneurs to learn and to thrive. I have worked with a quite a few intrapreneurs at large companies; people that have all of the autonomy of any independent entrepreneur plus the added benefit of prompt and substantial payment for services.

As an aside, there is one thing that I do have to warn you about going back, even temporarily, to work for a company after owning an entrepreneurial venture. You should be aware that many companies hold negative predispositions toward ex-entrepreneurs. They are often seen as uncommitted, dubious individuals who are primarily seeking to extract proprietary information and going off to profit from it. This viewpoint is, well........*misguided* (to put it nicely). *Thieves s*teal confidential information from employers, not ex-entrepreneurs. I consider them to be mutually exclusive! An entrepreneur has about the same chances of becoming a thief as an engineer, doctor, lawyer or any other profession. Now, the good news is that not all companies share this viewpoint. As a matter of fact, I can confidently submit that the majority do not; but many do. So if you do decide to take a job post-exit, please be aware of this mindset. If you encounter seemingly illogical reservations from a prospective employer; simply go to the next one; because they likely don't trust you and never will.

So, with regard to taking a job, I have to admit that I was somewhat reluctant to venture back to working for someone else having been on my own for so long. However, I chose to look at the situation in two ways. First, it was temporary; just something to keep my skills sharp before I decided on my next entrepreneurial goal. Second, having endured the rigors of self-employment, I felt that I was now much better employee than I was before. As a result of having run a successful business for so long, I found that I had gained a much more holistic perspective on organizations than I had in the past. For example, I could now clearly see the critical impact, such as the contribution to equity that each individual employee had or didn't have on a business. That was *NOT* the case before I was a full time entrepreneur. One of the most valuable lessons that I learned as an entrepreneur was that your vocation (entrepreneur or employee) should never be looked upon as *just* a source of income. I believe that beyond the satisfaction and pride of being paid for a job well done, the greatest aspects of working as an employee are the *unlimited* opportunities to meet a diverse array of interesting people, sharpen your business skills and learn about business as you see it unfold right before your eyes. As an employee, you have the opportunity to learn in real time about numerous business processes, such as, business strategy, economics, accounting, decision-making and organizational behavior. They are fantastic training grounds for future entrepreneurs and even better arenas for intrapreneurs to demonstrate their business savvy.

So, after wrapping up my involvement with the microbrewery, in addition to taking on a temporary job, I decided to *shake things up* a bit by going on a rigorous skills improvement regime; which I highly recommend doing. To begin this process, I reflected back on what I believed were my strongest and my weakest skills (see SWOT analysis later) during the time that I was running the brewery. I concluded that I had lacked a really deep understanding of how to streamline and proficiently run manufacturing processes *on a world-class level*. Additionally, I recognized that I was lacking fundamental knowledge of formal business principles. I concluded that if I could address these skills deficiencies, then I could make my next venture an even greater success than the brewery had been. To address these weaknesses, I decided to do an entrepreneurship-focused MBA and a very challenging Lean Six Sigma Black Belt program. Both of these programs provided me with cutting-edge tools for assessing new business concepts and for implementing dramatic improvements to existing business processes. So, with my formal business training and with my experience in building and running successful businesses, I set the course for my next goal, business process improvement. Today, I work as a business process improvement specialist and a small business start-up expert. My job is to find inefficient, ineffective processes proposed within a business concept or within an active business and find ways to turn them around. With the greatest amount of autonomy, I apply my knowledge and experiences to create significant value for companies. I identify incongruities and/or redundancies along the value chain and eliminate them, which is *really* profitable for the company. Best of all, it is still fun, and it still doesn't feel like "a job".

Keys to Success

When I think back on the effort that it took to work on a master's degree, a lean six sigma black belt, a full time job *and* raising a young family concurrently, it leads me to an important, no – make that a *fundamental* reason for this book: *tenacity* and *focus*. In my opinion, these two qualities, or more accurately, *skills*, will carry you further than almost any others. I'm not special, but over time I have *learned* to apply them well. You absolutely will need to develop both of these skills too if you are starting a small business or expecting to make a solid go of an existing one. Believe me when I tell you, it takes unbridled determination and commitment to see it through. I have no doubt that anyone can achieve anything desired, provided they have a *deep-felt reason* - the catalyst that makes it so. Find *the* reason why you want to take on a major challenge and use the passion that you have for your idea to build a fire in your belly and then, with laser-like precision; unleash. *That is focus.* Next, stay the course, no matter what. Let *nothing or no one* distract you from your objective. *That is tenacity.*

The sum of all my experiences and accrued knowledge has been put into this book. So, let's return to the original point, *"who is Cameron D. Howe and what can I expect to gain from reading this book?"* Well, I believe that I have addressed the first question. The answer to the second question is: *Value.*

Value in mistakes not made: Learning from the mistakes that I or others have made and turning those mistakes to your advantage.

Value in opportunities identified: Acquiring the ability to thoroughly analyze a potential business and to know ahead of time whether to venture in or move on.

Value in education: Having a robust set of analytical tools to effectively manage and optimize business processes and to render sound, fact-based resolutions to the daily problems that you will encounter.

Value in mitigating risk: In business risk is universal, but you will learn how to manage it rather than to fear it.

The value of experience: Let other people make mistakes and hit dead ends while you quietly do the right thing. That is the benefit and the value of experience.

The value of understanding the process – profit connection: You will understand the need to plan all of your processes for efficiency first. From routine clerical activities to full-scale production lines, an efficiency-first mindset must prevail. Waste is not an option. That means excessive inventory is not an option, idle employees is not an option, rework and excessive work in progress is not an option, low process yields is not an option. You will reduce your costs of non-conformance to virtually nil if you steadfastly apply the approaches that I present.

To provide this value, I begin by presenting a basic grounding in business terms and concepts - I *strongly* believe that you need to "speak the language" of business to be in business. Next, I move on to discuss specific details about my experiences of running businesses. Experiences like none that you'll find in any other business book. I present real-world trials and tribulations, not transcriptions from a strategy or finance textbook, but truly from the trenches examples. Experiences varying from *actually* managing finances, operations and quality assurance, to managing unadulterated madness! I can't help but to reminisce about the several times that our brewery's delivery truck was stolen (poor process). Or the time that I proudly designed and constructed a support frame for a beer tank only to discover that it was *a little* too big to take out of the room that it was built in and had to be cut in half and re-welded later (exceptionally poor process). Or the time that we decided to completely rebrand the business *one month before* the grand opening (risky process)! Good times? In hindsight yes, easy to laugh at now, not so much back then I have to admit. Just the tip of the iceberg I assure you.

So, back to the original point at the outset of this section; *what can this book do for me*? Well, *Control Your Processes...Control Your Profits* evolved out of decades of small business operations and big business exposure and represents the sum of my education and experiences in establishing and optimizing processes. It will give you real-world insight on the day-to-day aspects of running a business and it will help you to avoid what has been widely accepted as a rite of passage into the world of business, both large and small: stepping headlong into the myriad of bear traps just waiting for a fresh new ankle. It doesn't have to be this way and the key to avoiding these bear traps is through education; which is where we are going right now. Open your mind; it's time to learn.

Chapter 2 – Entrepreneurial Attitude

"You learn nothing from your successes except to think too much of yourself. It is from failure that all growth comes, provided you can recognize it, admit it, learn from it, rise above it, and then try again"

Dee Hock – Founder and Former CEO, VISA International

I congratulate you on your interest in starting a business or wanting to improve the one that you already own. Be assured that I am most humbled by having the opportunity to play a small part in this incredible process. Over the years, I have worked with many people who have experienced what you're feeling. I have felt it too; the magical calling of entrepreneurship, which is a curious mix of boundless energy, enthusiasm, empowerment, intrigue, freedom and hopefully a healthy dose of trepidation. All of this is normal and is, in fact, part of the reason that many people start businesses. The important thing is that you have decided to pursue something new.

Unfortunately, the natural response that many people feel when faced with an entrepreneurial calling is to deny it. They tell themselves that entrepreneurship is only for business-educated people, people with the right connections, people from a wealthy family, people born with *the gift*. Well, I am glad to tell you that all of this is patently false! When I started my various companies, I was lacking every one of these advantages and yet, there was no way that I was going to let that stop me.

It has been shown time and time again that the keys to successful entrepreneurship include:

- tenacity and focus; a "never give up" attitude with a burning desire to succeed

- a deep insight and understanding of a chosen market

- thoroughness of planning and preparation

- the ability to rein in resources (Note: I did not say *own* the resources)

- ability to manage the inevitable unknowns and unknowables

- flexibility and nimbleness

- ingenuity and creativity

- a sense of humor to see you through the tough times (optional, but can really help)

- the ability to assemble a quality, *trustworthy* team

- being honest and forthright

- a marketable new idea or an innovative spin on an old

idea – simply put; an idea that fulfills a need

- relentless enthusiasm, which is decidedly contagious to your team members

The more of *these* factors you possess….the better will be your chances of success. Now, notice that I did say *chances* of success, which leads me to the part of entrepreneurship that most people seem to be determined to ignore: failure. Call me the devil's advocate, but I won't omit the potential downside of starting your own business; the specter of failure. You may have heard that some alarming percentage of new businesses will fail. The most common figure that I hear being cited is about 80% ultimately succumb. That statistic might be accurate; however, it only considers part of the truth. It doesn't address the degree of preparation, determination and engagement of the entrepreneurs that succeeded versus the one's that failed. It doesn't consider the strategic alignment of the entrepreneur's background to their chosen market. It doesn't consider the knowledge, decision making skills or flexibility of the entrepreneurs that did well. These are *very* important considerations that should not be glossed over by simply asserting that four out of five will fail! Maybe four out of five *well-prepared* entrepreneurs succeed. I contend that a statistic damming 80% of future start-ups to failure, based on history, is irrelevant without being accompanied by a detailed profile of who failed, why they failed and how they failed. When I said "how" they failed, I am indicating that failure comes in a variety of forms. I would like to put the 80% figure behind us now and come up with definitions of what failure means and what it doesn't.

Failure doesn't necessarily have to refer to outright bankruptcy, because within a business context, failure comes in many forms. For our needs, I have distilled failure into three basic groups: *The setback, Caught in the Doldrums* and *The Epic Fail.*

The Setback:

Although I'm reluctant to frame it this way, if "The Setback" had to be described using the word "failure" then I would be inclined to call it a "good failure". Beyond being one heck of an oxymoron, good failure refers to believing that you have found the opportunity of a lifetime but paradoxically, choosing not to pursue it.

The Setback begins when you invest your heart and soul into a business idea, thoroughly going through the market research and due-diligence stages and in the end *logically and rationally* concluding that the project may not be as promising as you had hoped. Therefore, you very reluctantly abort your plans to start the business. Though it may feel like a failure, especially if many people are let down by your decision, take it from me, this is not a failure – if you are a true entrepreneur, then this is only a setback. If this has been your experience, then I commend you on making an extremely difficult decision, but a good one indeed. You should not be discouraged; disappointed to be sure, but that is understandable. As a true entrepreneur you will be back again with new ideas and eventually one of these ideas will pass the due-diligence stage and move on to a start-up. The important lesson to be gleaned from this scenario is that you had sufficient confidence in your analyses to trust your own conclusions and act upon them. For some, this level of discipline is never achieved. Be assured that this ability will serve you well once you do start a business. Consider it a minor setback in the big picture and start the process again.

Caught in the Doldrums:

Caught in the Doldrums refers to having a business that is already operating and viable but is just not terribly successful *and never will be*. I am referring to businesses that languish for years, never growing appreciably but merely existing to cover expenses (and hopefully a salary) with little or nothing left over to contribute to equity. In short, what the owner has accomplished is the creation of nothing more than a job. Now, some may consider the creation of your own job to be a huge success, and if that is your goal then that is great. However, you should be forewarned that this is an excruciatingly difficult path to that goal. Within the risk/reward paradigm, owners of such a business may have taken on a significant debt load and paid substantial personal costs, for example; low wages, little or no retirement savings, poor or no benefits and vacations? What vacations!!? What is even worse is that over the long term these owners will probably build up very little equity. I have seen this many times before and it is never fun for the business owner, especially once they realize that there is virtually no "clean" way to exit the business. There is usually no profitable exit strategy available because the owner has not created true value and if there was ever a truism in business, it is this: *no one is going to buy a business that is lacking in book value and/or potential for significant future value.* Therefore, for the poor entrepreneur, it is preferable on one hand, to stay in business (from a capital-investment loss perspective – also called *barrier to exit*) and at the same time, it is preferable to get out of the business (from a personal cost and opportunity cost perspective) – an *entrepreneur's paradox* that you should avoid like the plague. So what to do? Some may argue that the owner can simply walk away from this type of business and get a job. There are two big problems with this theory:

1) The aforementioned example of the entrepreneur's paradox

2) Securing employment

Once you have ventured out on your own, as we touched on before, going back to employment can be a dubious undertaking. The point is, your transition back to employee status will take longer and will prove much more challenging than normal. So, before venturing out on your own you must ensure that you have a solid, proven business model, business case and business plan to execute and that you fully understand and have mitigated as much of the downside risk as possible. If your business model allows you to test the success potential of the business *before* committing wholesale, that is best. Online business models that don't infringe in any way upon your responsibilities to your employer's business (ethics first) and that can be worked on during your free time would fall into this category.

The Epic Fail

The worst for last; the epic fail. The epic fail refers to situations where a would-be entrepreneur has a business idea that would most appropriately fall into the category of "The Setback". Instead of doing the right thing and walking away from a flawed idea, he **_foolishly_** chooses to pursue it. So rather than investigating time and resources into a viable project, the overzealous individual opts with a "damn the torpedoes" approach and pushes forward with the start-up. He believes mistakenly that he can fix the *fundamental* problems identified in due diligence. Note that virtually all good business opportunities will have minor flaws, but NOT fundamental ones! An example of a fundamentally flawed small business model would be one that proposes to compete profitably on price point with Walmart – sorry, but not a chance! Another example would be an entrepreneur who wants to invest his life savings in a restaurant located in the same place where four other restaurants have failed previously. Emotions can be deadly in business. Under the Epic Fail scenario, one dramatically increases the risk of losing his or her entire investment in time and money if fundamental flaws are ignored. Most importantly, consider this: Did they resign from their job? What will be the toll on their marriage or on their children? What about opportunity costs? Did they miss the chance to pursue a truly profitable venture? It gets worse. If the unlucky owner of such a business compounded his/her woes by also making the fatal mistake of not structuring the business appropriately to limit personal liability, then he/she could also lose other assets, such as, houses, cars and savings.

As intelligent entrepreneurs we need to define and commit to some basic ground rules when considering an investment in a business. Once you have established your business idea, you should conduct your due diligence as thoroughly as possible. Gather as much information as you can on the business model, the market, the location, the processes and any special knowledge required. Next, assess your business idea using the *eight entrepreneurial tests* - which we will learn about later. As a rule of thumb, make sure that your analyses are as quantitative/numbers driven as possible. It is very hard to protest against numbers that show a complete non-starter. Be aware of the fact that emotions and ego *will* put limits on your capacity to remain unbiased when conducting your analyses. This is where a third party becomes a necessity. Be prepared to allow at least one other person who has substantial business acumen, such as an experienced management consultant, to critique your plan. You might be amazed by what a third party can see that you may have missed. Once I was asked to vet a major expansion plan for a manufacturing business and I came across an oversight in the plan that *to me* was so glaring and substantial that the project would have been an outright failure if left uncorrected. Worse, if the project had been completed per the plan, there would have been no cost efficient way to remedy or re-engineer the problems later! I was absolutely amazed that none of the six project team members, the consulting engineer or the equipment company that did the process design and business case saw the mistake. Even the fellow who was writing the cheque for almost $2,000,000 to fund the project had missed it! Yikes!

Remember, even in cases where the financial analyses indicate that your idea has significant upside, one still takes on risk during a start-up. Multiply that risk by orders of magnitude when your analyses indicate that you don't have a winner on your hands. ***Walk away from marginal, fundamentally flawed business ideas; Do not start up!***

The Fine Line between Failure and Success

Before moving on, I would like to encourage you with a few anecdotes from some of the most inspiring leaders that have ever lived and their perspectives on failure. While these examples do not necessarily deal with entrepreneurship directly, the moral of each story is applicable to any entrepreneur's situation, because entrepreneurs are, by default, leaders.

Abraham Lincoln, the 14th president of the United States, secured his place in history as "The Great Emancipator", amongst many other distinctions, through the abolishment of slavery in the United States. President Lincoln achieved much in his lifetime; however, the road to his success was paved with repeated setbacks and much tragedy. Some of the notable events during Lincoln's life were:

- 1831 lost his job

- 1832 he failed in politics

- 1833, his second business failed

- 1835 his fiancée died

- 1838 he sought the position of speaker of the state legislator and lost

- 1843 he failed to win his party's nomination to run for Congress

- 1846 Ran for Congress and won

- 1860, he ran for the President of the United States and won

Can you imagine the fortitude that Lincoln must have developed to be able to rise from the ashes of repeated, sometimes tragic failure, to eventually hold one of the highest offices in the free world? Truly inspiring. So, as you move from phase to phase in your entrepreneurial endeavors, you may want to think often about how Abraham Lincoln must have felt after each setback and how he put each one behind and pressed on. Building and running a business is not an undertaking for the meek so from time to time you will need to tap into this kind of strength and fortitude to stay the course.

Another great leader of the past, Sir Winston Churchill, the Prime Minister of England during World War II, was credited with saying: *"Success is the ability to go from failure to failure without losing your enthusiasm"*. Churchill was a pillar of strength during the war effort, and with that strength he played a key role in leading the allies to victory. As an example of this you need to look no further than the horrific black and white reels of the massive rubble pile that London had become through relentless German bombing juxtaposed with Churchill's chilling and inspiring words:

"We shall fight in France, we shall fight on the seas and oceans, we shall fight with growing confidence and growing strength in the air, we shall defend our island, whatever the cost may be. We shall fight on the beaches, we shall fight on the landing grounds, we shall fight in the fields and in the streets, we shall fight in the hills; we shall never surrender".

Failure was not an option for Churchill.

Both Churchill and Lincoln were the embodiment of wisdom, tenacity and strength and an obvious commonality between them was that *nothing* was going to stop them from achieving their goals. While these anecdotes of success triumphing over failure may be inspiring, to some, this focus on failure may seem somewhat disheartening. My point is to embrace failure as a *possible* "price to pay" along the road to success. And if you do fail, I implore you to dust yourself off and push on to success, because it is NOT my intention to prepare you to proceed from failure to failure. On the contrary, I want to see you succeed in grand fashion *the first time*. To achieve first-time success, I believe that you should reject that traditional trial and error approach to entrepreneurship and adopt a methodology that is both wiser and *far* less painful: *acquiring knowledge and understanding from <u>other people's failures.</u>* So when you see a vacant unit that was once a restaurant, this apparent failure provides a good indicator of why you would want to avoid setting up a restaurant at that location. Sounds obvious right? Well, I can't begin to tell you how many times that I have seen this rule broken and in the end guess what happens? The same business model, situated at the same location, fails again.

So, let failures belong to other people and you make sure that you learn from them. I can assure you that this will save you time, money and much heartache. The entrepreneur who ignores unfavorable due diligence and proceeds to start up regardless has chosen a perilous path and more often than not is fittingly rewarded with failure.

Learning from other peoples failures doesn't give you permission to become complacent or to lose your focus and tenacity. You *will* need to focus more than you likely ever have before. So, with this focus, a vision of your future business in mind and this book in hand, you will have set out onto a voyage with a map in hand. Let's move onto a case study to get some real world insight on a start-up.

Chapter 3 – Case Study: Salinas Valley Custom Wines

"Exercise caution in your business affairs; for the world is full of trickery"

Desiderata

In my humble opinion, too many books on entrepreneurship delve into overly detailed analyses, scholarly platitudes and philosophies to such an extent that chewing glass would be more enjoyable then reading them.   Now please don't misinterpret my sarcasm as a knock on business theory, because I do believe that theory and philosophy are decidedly of value, *but in reasonable doses and within context*.   In this book I do things a little differently...no, actually a *lot* differently. I present what I believe is a balanced, anecdote-based approach to starting a business, stemming from my own practical experiences and my education. This does not mean that you are completely off the hook with regard to theory (says he smiling!) because this book is actually brimming with it.   The difference is that the theory that I will present is of a far more practical and useful nature than standard business philosophies, which I prefer to leave to the scholars. Also, I have done my best to temper this theory with relevant examples to further emphasize the message. The presentation of the following case is a good example.

You are about to read a case study about the experiences of a group of friends that started a wine company. I believe that you will find the impact of this case to be profound. It focuses on the dangers of a grassroots approach to establishing a business and it also demonstrates the caustic effects of greed run amuck. In short, it will provide you with much greater insight on business start-ups than studying esoteric theories on organizational behavior and team dynamics. So, what we will do is examine this very important case, drawing out salient points and emphasizing the importance and relevance of each. Since much of my professional background is in the alcohol beverage industry, I thought it fitting to source a case study about a business operating in that segment. Note, due to confidentiality issues, aliases have been used in lieu of the actual names. The important thing of course is not the names, but the lessons flowing from the events and how they can be applied to your particular situation.

Case Study: Salinas Valley Custom Wines

Part I

This case is a prime example of bootstrapping taken to the extreme. It is the story of an inexperienced, naive team with good ideas and intentions that were squandered by poor decision making, lack of formal business knowledge and most of all, lack of working capital. Study this case very carefully. It could save you untold amounts of grief, lost time and money.

Salinas Valley Custom Wines (SVCW) is a specialty wine producer that is still in existence today in a location between Salinas and San Jose, California. SVCW was conceived of between two friends, Mike and Steve, who coincidentally, were both released from their respective full-time Silicon Valley companies during the very same week.

Mike and Steve had always talked about starting a company, but as is so common, they lacked a marketable idea and had almost always been wearing golden handcuffs too. So, with both pairs of golden handcuffs now removed, they met at Mike's house, sat down in the kitchen and began brainstorming ideas for a business start-up. During their meeting, they happened upon Steve's passion for making unique tasting wines. Steve had received spectacular feedback from his family and friends about his wines; they frequently suggested that he consider opening a boutique winery; especially since they were surrounded by Californian wine country. Steve and Mike were very intrigued by the idea of a new winery. They reasoned that they had only to find a good location and to scale up Steve's current tiny process, and then they would be able to sell endless amounts of wine - simple....

Enthusiasm took over. The pair had what both believed would be a great, marketable idea and they were determined to pursue it. The market research conducted by the pair, beyond feedback from friends, was somewhat limited. This research consisted of phone calls to acquaintances that were working at small wineries, visits to local wineries and Internet-based research on large wineries. No attempt was made to seek detailed, geographic-specific market data and the reasons for this were twofold. First, their limited cash was earmarked as operating capital and not, as Steve put it, to be *"squandered on demographics"*. Second, they had read and heard *"countless news stories"* about double-digit growth for Californian niche wine producers; so they believed that formalized market research would be pointless – especially considering that they lived in a *"winery cornucopia"*. Effectively, they were sold on the idea before they even finished the due diligence stage.

Analysis: Two possible missteps were made right out of the gate. Clearly, the main reason that Steve and Mike chose to investigate a start-up was because they both needed jobs. The *primary* motivating factor was *not* building a scalable and saleable business but creating a job. This can be problematic. Solving unmet needs should always be the *primary* motivator for starting a new venture. I can think of no exception to this. Solving unmet needs invariably leads to the creation of value and one must strive to create value in a business because:

1. It is your perquisite to the option of "cashing out" and exiting later on

2. The equity in a business can be used to leverage other businesses or simply left as a legacy to be passed along as you see fit

There is no substitute for *professionally executed* formal market research when starting a business. "Cheeping out" in this regard can be deadly. Accepting praise from well-meaning friends and family as a substitute for value-added research was a major misstep made by the team. While approval from friends and family is flattering, it should *never* form the primary basis for starting a business: If you do this, then you do so at your own peril. You require professional input to properly analyze your business idea. Think of this saying when you set up your business: "if you think it's expensive to hire a professional to do the job, wait until you see what an amateur costs". So try your very best to get at least *some* professional input in this regard. Even pay for a bit of advice on what you can complete on your own – you might save 50 to 75% of the cost and still reap most of the benefits. While enthusiasm and optimism are generally very constructive, they are decidedly not when they bias market research, or worse substitute for it. Biasing research by gravitating towards reasons to start up, while playing down reasons not to start up is always a huge mistake. Balance must be sought between these two equally important, but opposite objectives, which are:

- Finding good reason to pursue an opportunity

- Finding any reason to run from an opportunity!

Time for a sports analogy! Think of the complimentary yet disparate objectives of a football team's offense and defense. The offense's primary role is to advance or progress while the defense's primary role is to mitigate or protect. Your research and due diligence methodology requires a similarly balanced and contrasted approach. Never forget: reason *before* passion.

Case Study: Salinas Valley Custom Wines

Part II

Six months went by and in that time, the pair continued planning their business. To their credit, they were pragmatic enough to realize that they were not capable of running the new business entirely on their own. They reached out to family members to see if anyone might be interested in playing a part in the business. Steve's cousin, Paul, an accomplished marketer had expressed interest in the venture. Paul's wife, Annette was a very outgoing "people" person and she too had expressed interest in the business, particularly sales. The team was now formed and ready to go.

The Business Plan

Steve and Mike were planning to enquire at a local bank about the possibility of receiving a small business loan for equipment purchases. To their credit, they understood that without a formal business plan in hand they would have a huge credibility gap in the eyes of their banker, so they started writing.

The business plan covered that following subjects:

- **Market and Competition** – major local competitors and

their respective good and bad points. Potential customers were identified. The total market value was identified.

- **Sales and Revenues projections** – estimates for sales were made; but were very much contrived.

- **Required assets and property** – a list of all equipment that was needed as well as the size of the property required.

- **Marketing and advertising** – Paul's plan for a guerilla marketing and advertising campaign along with various PR plans.

- **The Team** - detailed description of each member's skills, background and role to be played in the company. The relative equity percentage that each core team member would possess.

- **Finance** – the exact amount of paid-in working capital from each shareholder, loan requirements for equipment and leasehold improvements

Mike and Steve finished the business plan and then approached the bank. To their utter astonishment (times were tough for getting funding for start-ups) they received the bank's blessing and they secured a small business loan. So, despite having no formalized experience in their chosen industry or experience running a business, they got the financing in place and pushed forward with the plan.

Marketing & Positioning Strategy

With Paul's strong background in marketing and advertising, he created the product logo, corporate colors, the company catch phrase, point-of-purchase materials, brochures and grand opening plans.

Building the Plant

For over six months Steve designed the plant and specified the new equipment that would need to be purchased. For the rest of the equipment requirements, Steve had sourced quality used items, which saved the team a significant amount of money.

It took some time to find and secure a good location, and then several months more to get leasehold improvements completed. The improvements included the installation of a massive cooling system, drainage, increased power, signs, an on-premise retail store, a lounge area for tours and back office space. For many months equipment was brought into the facility and integrated. By the ninth month, the plant was ready to be commissioned.

Up and running

Once the plant was commissioned, the difficult task of precisely scaling up Steve's recipes began. The process was very technical and involved significant trial and error, which unfortunately, resulted in substantial material loss. Regrettably, it was necessary to discard the first three 1500 gallon batches of wine due to quality issues. The effects of these problems were exacerbated by the fact that there were absolutely no revenues yet. Furthermore, beyond substantial raw material losses, cash was being burned on overheads and debt service at an alarming rate. This deadly duo of cash burning in combination with little or no revenues leads to a net negative cash flow that is very appropriately referred to as *the Valley of Death* (see diagram below).

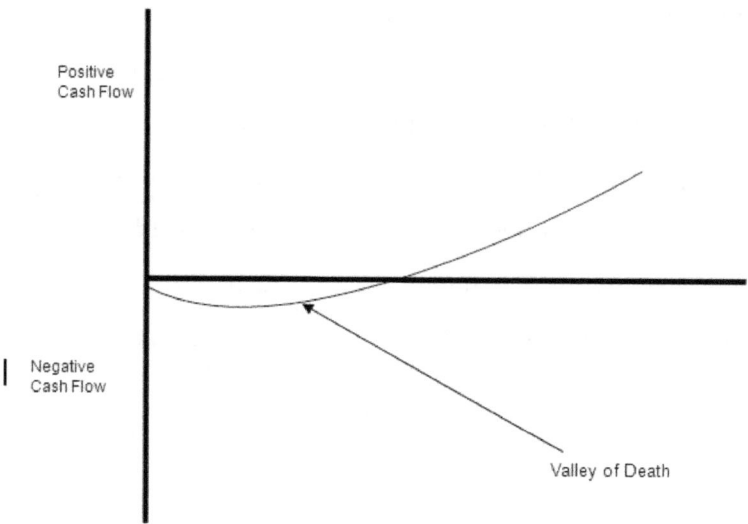

Valley of Death Cash Flow Model

Another contributing issue to the profit lag was the time required for the wines to complete fermentation and aging, which technically required *months*. To hasten this process, Steve deliberately allowed some of the first batches of wine to ferment and age at higher temperatures; a dubious practice that halved the maturation time but at the risk of potentially affecting the quality of the wine negatively. He believed that the difference in the wine profile would be so negligible that only the most sensitive palate would notice. Steve justified the quality compromise by reasoning that getting any sales at this point would be much better than waiting for another month to go by and risk bankruptcies.

Analysis: Entry into the valley of death begins once you spend your first penny without a revenue stream to replace it. The above figure might seem to imply that once a business thankfully escapes the valley of death, that it is home free. This is not necessarily a given. As you will see later, multiple dips into the valley are possible and obviously something that you really want to avoid. In your venture, constantly be aware of the valley of death. Absolutely justify all expenses and if you can "cost efficiently" avoid an expenditure using a bootstrapped approach, then do it. Also, do your best to make sure that unavoidable expenses are aligned with your revenues and overall strategy no matter how difficult that may be. In the case of the SVCW, more seasoned entrepreneurs likely would have been better prepared for this phase of the business in two ways:

1) Having reasonable cash reserves set aside to endure the valley of death

2) Having more thoroughly understood and prepared for revenue lags associated with recipe scale-up and the wine aging process

I can't emphasize the following point enough: Steve's unilateral decision to compromise on quality in order to hasten the flow of sales revenues could be considered one of the biggest blunders made by any one of the team members. Customers become *and remain* customers for one simple reason: *value*. Steve's decision to speed up the fermentation process had the potential to eat through the company's value proposition like a cancer. Please, do not *ever* compromise the quality or value of your product to make up for inadequacies in your planning process. Do have back-up resources in place for such an event or better yet, be more meticulous in your planning before you start up. Failing that, if you do find yourself in a similar situation and you haven't planned any back-up resources, suck it up and go find more money (i.e. sell *some* ownership!) to float the business until you can offer the very best quality product/service. The return on this investment is huge and potentially a game saver for a business.

Case Study: Salinas Valley Custom Wines

Part III

Post Start-up

The market acceptance of SVCW's first products was reasonably positive, despite the quality risks that were taken with product aging, and as a result, demand grew very quickly. Even though the team started the business to be as successful as possible, ironically they were woefully unprepared for success when it came. Quickly they found themselves in a situation where they lacked the capital, financial, physical and human, to produce enough wine to meet the growing demand. The result was stock-outs at stores, distributors and restaurants. The resulting losses in revenues left the company drifting along in the valley of death with a depleting reserve of working capital. The net effect of these stock-outs was reduced brand loyalty with customers, who simply migrated towards the brands that were consistently available. Given their situation, the partners concluded that they immediately needed to acquire more equipment to increase the plant's capacity. Unfortunately, the team had a big problem. With so much of their operating capital spent, the partners were not in a financial position to acquire new equipment; unless they were prepared to pledge personal assets such as their homes as collateral. As distasteful as it was, the choice almost made itself. They needed a partner. They reasoned that a partner could provide the much needed cash infusion for the financing of new equipment. Also, a new, *experienced* partner could also provide the business acumen that the team clearly lacked. On the positive side, they now had a proven product which would help them to attract a new partner. The partner that they decided upon was a friend of Steve's and her name was Lisa. Steve and Lisa met as undergraduates at university and managed to stay in touch. Steve had a significant amount of respect for Lisa and her business savvy because she had built and sold several companies since she had graduated from an Ivy League business school. When Lisa met with the team, they discussed the current financial condition of the company, the marketplace potential and the product portfolio. The partners believed that the market awareness and acceptance of the company's products had reached a tipping point and that a financial investment would be the catalyst to help push the company into profitability.

In the end, there was consensus to sell a 30% stake of the company to Lisa. With the cash injection that Lisa provided in return for the shares, new equipment was purchased immediately which doubled the plant's output capacity. From that point, with demand increasing steadily, revenues began to climb and the valley of death was left behind. To ensure that plant capacity moved in lockstep with increasing demand, much of the profit was reinvested into the business to buy more equipment. In addition to incurring costs for equipment purchases, at the companies eighteenth month of existence the group voted to allow Mike and Steve, the only two full-time employees, to begin drawing small salaries.

As the years marched on the company's revenues continued to grow, however only slightly exceeding costs to yield a negligible profit. By the fourth year the physical space within the plant was at such a premium that production capacity was constrained. The partners concluded that moving to a new facility was not an option, given the fact that they had established a brisk walk-in clientele. Also, since the company had made a substantial investment in leasehold improvements at the current facility and had very good proximity to the city, the partners concluded that the only option was to expand the current facility. There was a major problem with this plan, however. The expansion would require a huge influx of money to finance - close to 1.5 times the company's annual revenues. The unabated need to constantly reinvest in new equipment made the company quite cash poor. It was at this point that Lisa, a very well-heeled entrepreneur, offered to secure financing for the building expansion and the acquisition of more capital assets in exchange for the purchase of majority shares. The deal, as she saw it, would end up giving her a total of 51% ownership of the company. As the original partners considered the offer, they experienced mixed feelings. If they accepted Lisa's offer, they would be content knowing that the SVWC was likely going to survive. On the other hand they were uncomfortable with losing control of the company that they had worked so hard to build. They discussed it almost continuously over the next month and in the end decided to sell majority interest to Lisa. After all, they reasoned, they trusted her.

Improved facility

Along with accruing the costs associated with the building addition, the company had purchased a significant amount of equipment in order to meet, what Lisa expected to be, significantly increased demand. To create this demand, Lisa had hired four new employees into the key roles in sales, strategy, production and customer service. These employees came from her other companies. Unfortunately, these new employees had no prior experience in the Californian wine business and no specific experience in their respective functional areas. The original partners couldn't understand what she was trying to accomplish. With so much riding on the need for higher demand due to increased overheads, leasehold improvements, debt service and four new salaries, Lisa's strategy seemed preposterous. Her intentions in hiring these employees were later confirmed duplicitous after Steve made an unfortunate discovery. He found out, unequivocally that the new employees had been instructed to act surreptitiously as emissaries on Lisa's behalf and report back to her the daily activities at the winery, including the activities of her partners! Needless to say, previous assumptions that Steve had made about the trustworthiness of his friend Lisa were now in question.

The expanded plant was commissioned and running. However, with the significantly increased debt load and lagging sales, the company's cash position was once again being stressed. It seemed that virtually no progress had been made on the sales or strategy front. Accordingly, the lack of competence of the new employees was being raised constantly by the original partners. Steve was becoming so frustrated with Lisa and the arrogance and indifference that she seemed to be displaying towards her partners that he decided to put on his detective cap. What Steve had found out effectively connected all of the dots in the mystery that the company had become. He discovered that the employees that Lisa had hired were all cast-outs from her other companies – her important companies. At that point, it became crystal clear to Steve that Lisa had been using SVCW as a repository for failed and incompetent employees. By shifting their employment to the winery, Lisa dodged legal issues associated with termination by giving the cast-outs a new job and, at the same time, protecting her main businesses from the problems of incompetence. This was a win-win situation for Lisa, though not so much for the winery.

Despite Lisa's theories, demand did not spike as she had expected. The cash account was negative again, well into the upper limit of the line of credit. Creditors were being forced to wait 60 to 90 days for payment, as opposed to 30 days when the business was run by the original partners. In a misguided attempt to adopt "lean" production practices and to save cash,

Lisa insisted that all future raw material inventories were to be held in very low supply. As a consequence, on more than one occasion, this resulted in the cancellation of wine batches and packaging runs due to lack of materials. It was apparent to the founders that the company was now in an all-out tailspin. When Lisa was questioned about her various strategies by the partners, she lashed out at them, blaming them for the company's poor performance. Whenever they questioned Lisa about the competence of the new employees, she became enraged and threatened to pull the plug on the venture. It seemed to everyone involved that in the time that Lisa had been given full control of the company, she had transformed from a true, trusted partner into a duplicitous, scheming authoritarian. Paul's recommendations for PR events, advertisements, and promotions were summarily dismissed by her; if she responded at all. Paul wanted the company logo and images of their merlot bottle/label painted on their delivery trucks, since the trucks were all through the Bay area each week and in full view of thousands of people. Lisa took exception to this idea and told Paul that she knew everything that there was to know about advertising and that painting the trucks would be of no value. She went on to say that advertising was not even needed in the wine business and to create sales all that they needed to do was to *"just get people to try the wine"*. Paul and Lisa ceased to communicate with each other after that conversation.

Steve became more and more concerned as time progressed and the relationship between Lisa and the other partners eroded. Steve was determined to find out why she had become so overtly aggressive with her partners. Although he didn't want to believe it, he suspected that Lisa was making a play to take the entire company. It seemed to him that Lisa's first step to doing that was by thoroughly alienating herself with the other partners. Steve sent emails and left voice mails and requested meetings with Lisa and received no response. He sent emails and left messages asking to see the company's financial statements for the last few years and got no response. The original partners were well aware of the fact that since Lisa had assumed control of the company, financial statements were never seen by anyone but Lisa, despite numerous requests by Steve. After much reflection, Steve concluded that Lisa had purchased the company - actually closer to a leveraged buyout financed through her other companies - as a tax incentive; because, as many accountants will tell you, *sometimes* having an audited loss on one hand can be very beneficial for the other hand. All accounting magic aside, what was very clear to Steve was that the company was Lisa's dumping ground for her rejected employees from her other businesses. The founders realized that Lisa was a player with an agenda. She clearly was planning to slowly but absolutely take the entire company from her partners.

The original partners admitted that they had learned two valuable lessons the hard way. First, *never* let the appearance or the possessions (Ivy League education, cars, businesses, homes) of a person be your guide when judging their integrity. Second, and most importantly, *blind trust is for fools*.

The founders met with their lawyer and explained the situation. The lawyer indicated that the former partners were likely in the process of being "frozen out" of the business and that beyond leaving, there was little that they could do about it. Steve and Mike were devastated. The company was the culmination of their life's work and passion, and in the end; apparently it was just a game for Lisa. After much thought and deliberation, the pair sent Lisa their resignations. The founders walked away from the business and the lawyers for both sides started working overtime. In the end, Lisa got the entire company and the founders were paid out a paltry amount of money for their shares. If they didn't accept the offer for this money, Lisa implied that she was going to push the company into bankruptcy and then buy it outright from the receiver, leaving the original partners with nothing.

In hindsight, a huge misstep that the founders made was in not insisting on a "shot-gun clause" during negotiations of the new partnership agreement. A shot gun clause would have afforded the founders a mechanism to either buy Lisa out or get a much fairer valuation for their shares. Not too long after the original founders had left the business, Salinas Valley Custom Wines trucks began bearing the company logos and pictures of their Merlot bottles.

Once everything between Lisa and the former partners was concluded, something very interesting happened. During the time of the squabbles and strife between Lisa and the founders, new leaner and smarter wineries were getting established and making inroads into the market. Two years after the founders were effectively pushed from the business, the competition had eclipsed SVCW. One of these newer competitors had been selling ten to one compared to SVCW.

Analysis: When I learned of this story I was empathetic for the founders of SVCW, but I was not surprised because I have seen many "Lisa's" out there. Choosing a partner may be the most important decision that can be made, one that will literally make or break your business. Unfortunately, for most mortals who venture into capital-intensive businesses, the need for taking on a partner at some point is almost unavoidable, especially if you don't hit the ground running when the business opens. Expanding businesses *organically* - which means expansion that is financed from company-generated resources only, without borrowing - can take a very long time. Therefore, some form of financial assistance is often required. Aside from the remote possibility of a rich aunt bequeathing you five or ten million dollars, let's focus on the basic sources of financing; debt and equity. To be eligible for debt financing, rule one for virtually all lenders is that sufficient *liquid* assets must be pledged as collateral to secure the loans. Unfortunately, lenders usually will not consider allowing assets, such as equipment, inventories and even registered personal savings (401K, IRA, Personal Pension Scheme, RRSP) as eligible collateral against loans. Lenders want security in the form of unsecured liquid assets, such as houses, vacation homes, vehicles, land or cash, ironically. So the moral to the story is: If you need to find ways to further your company's growth *quickly*, you will either need to sell ownership of the business or you will need to borrow money. Remember though, you accept either of these choices at the risk of losing your business or your personal property, an unsavory dilemma to be sure. If you are nervous about putting all of your eggs into one basket by committing to a single financing source, you should probably go with your gut and seek numerous investors. However, be warned that finding multiple investors with liquid cash, especially lots of cash is generally pretty difficult to do. Also, there can be Securities implications depending on the number of investors, investor solicitation methods and investor qualification/sophistication.

In short, it gets complicated! For better or for worse, finding a couple of investors or more likely just one is much more probable in the end. Now here is the good news. *If done correctly*, taking on partners is a synergistic process, a relatively small sacrifice that leads to substantial long-term net gains for all parties involved. So, just how *do* you "do it correctly"? For starters, it is vital to that you heed your lawyer's recommendations in structuring a partnership agreement so that you don't risk losing everything that you have worked so hard to accomplish. The first step in this process is being very, *very* prepared when you are considering an investor and then actually going through a rigorous negotiation phase. Don't take a haphazard approach to this and please be prepared to sweat every single detail. Remember, this is not just your business: It is how you will be living your life, so you and your partner need to be happy in the end. Negotiating is a give and take process and like it or not, ego plays a substantial role in the process. So, when you are in negotiations please make sure that you have an assortment of "giveaways" - inconsequential bargaining chips that look impressive to the other party, mean little to you and that you are prepared to concede. Also, if you want certain perks written into the agreement, always ask for more than you really want. If you want four weeks of vacation written into the agreement, then negotiate hard for six and see where the dust settles. You might get six, you'll definitely get four.

The following topic *must be fully explored by you and your lawyer*: control of your company. Although this is not legal advice and definitely not a substitute for a conversation with your lawyer, here are my feelings on the subject. If you are amenable to selling control of your business (*please* try your very best NOT to if you can!) I implore you to pay very close attention to this next sentence. **Restrictive deals that stipulate the *exclusion* of critical items, such as *shotgun clauses* and include potentially problematic items such as *non-competition clauses* should not only be viewed with a jaundiced eye, but should be summarily rejected.** If you accept such an offer, you have not only given up control, you have also given up your remedies, your lifeline to rescue you from a bad partnership. You do not want to tie your hands and limit your employment options if you choose to exit or are frozen out; and that is exactly what a non-compete will do to you. This is very important. A bigger issue that I have with being presented with a "non-compete": I would be very leery of any partner who insisted on the inclusion of one because it is effectively paving my way out the door. It also indicates a level of distrust or duplicity on behalf of your partner. That said, if having a non-compete seems unavoidable, be aware of onerous geographical restrictions or very lengthy enforcement terms that will tie your hands either in finding work or landing you in a courtroom if you have no choice but to compete. As far as shotgun clauses go, if your prospective partner doesn't want one, I would not walk, *I would run away*. Shotgun clauses make pre-planned provisions for the unthinkable, *but possible*, which is partnership dissolution or more aptly a "divorce". You must prepare for a clean divorce should the partnership fail. If the original investors in the case study had insisted upon a shot gun clause, then perhaps Lisa would have been either bought out or the partners would have left with much more money in their pockets. Given Lisa's duplicitous intent, she would have likely refused to sign a shot gun agreement, which would have been a massive, waving red flag in the eyes of the partners and given them reasonable cause to dismiss her as a potential partner. Regardless of how "nice" you think your potential partner is, never trust him or her 100%, because you just can't rule out duplicity – you need to protect yourself, involve your lawyer completely, listen to your accountant, and to that tiny, pragmatic voice that lies inside you!

Another fundamental takeaway from this case is that capital intensive businesses, such as manufacturing companies, typically require very deep pockets. You don't necessarily need to avoid these business models, but you do need to consider how you are going to strike a balance between getting adequate funding while maintaining a reasonable level of ownership and rights post deal. In a well-structured partnership agreement, diluted equity does not necessarily have to mean diluted power. Look no further than Facebook's almost comical IPO and the deal that Mark Zuckerberg worked if you want to see an example of that.

This case study highlighted, in graphic detail, the downside of oil and water partnerships. If you are lucky and have the financial wherewithal (rich aunt), you will not *need* to take on a partner. However, if you do conclude that taking on a partner is unavoidable or perhaps desirable for whatever reason, beyond what I have already mentioned, do yourself a favor by heeding the following advice:

- fully explore and protect yourself from worst-case scenarios such as a freeze-outs or embezzlement; it can and does happen all the time

- try your best to never give up control of your company

- try to spread ownership over several partners rather than one if at all possible

- seek out angel investors

- heed these sage words from Warren Buffett: *"You can't* make a good deal with a bad person".

The Remedy

I believe that there was a different approach available to the team which they could have taken to make this a much happier story. They could have avoided all their woes and never needed Lisa as a partner by thinking laterally about how the company should have been started and grown. Pay particular attention to this if you intend on starting a manufacturing company. A better approach may have been to solicit the services of another winery with excess capacity and contract them to produce wines with Steve's guidance, on an ad-hoc basis. This approach would have allowed the team to pay only for raw materials, labour, markup and some expenses such as advertising and distribution. Not leasehold improvements, not overheads on a woefully underutilized plant, not debt service and not the salaries for ineffectual employees. After a few years of running in this manner, with established brands created and a healthy balance sheet, they could then begin exploring the economics of constructing a plant. The result: no Lisa and all of the baggage that came with her, no protracted periods of burning cash and best of all: options.

This will be addressed in much greater depth in both the Accounting section and the Pricing section of Marketing, but when considering a start-up, you should be very conservative when calculating revenues and costs (e.g. equipment costs, raw materials, overheads, debt service). As for cash-flow, it is very important to expect and to plan for a long stint in the valley of death. If this ends up not being the case then you're off to a great start. However, if you find yourself in this predicament, as many start-ups do, you will be very happy to have those cash reserves ready. As mentioned before, would-be entrepreneurs that are thinking about bootstrapping their venture are well advised to be particularly leery of high capital cost businesses. Also be aware of potentially onerous financial commitments related to businesses with large square footage, low inventory turnover ratios or high conversion costs (see Accounting Ratios section). All of these items represent a major pull on working capital, will keep you firmly entrenched in a negative cash-flow spiral and could eventually push your business into receivership. Plan carefully; minimize risk.

So, is this all bad news? Well for the founders of the SVCW it was not good, but for you, it is great news. This is the power of learning from other peoples failures. Now that you have lived a sliver of this team's nightmare, you are all the wiser and you won't make the same missteps that they did. Promise you won't and then let's move on!

Chapter 4 - Learning Materials for a Smoother Start-up

"An investment in knowledge pays the best interest"

Benjamin Franklin

I strongly believe that a critical skill needed to plan, build and manage a successful business is the ability to render logical, fact-based decisions; and to do it consistently. Good decision making requires knowledge and skill, both acquirable. Once you have acquired the requisite knowledge and skill, you will be able to cut through layers of ambiguity and uncertainty to unearth the root cause of a problem and address it. If you believe that your business knowledge is lacking, please don't let this intimidate you in the least because we are going to spend a considerable amount of time developing it. When we are finished this section you will have significantly more business knowledge than I had when I became a full time entrepreneur. Examples of situations that your new or improved skills will help you address are:

- negotiating agreements and contracts such as the purchase/lease of property, equipment or vehicles; supplier contracts; negotiating with customers

- understanding economics and how it affects small businesses

- understanding how price elasticity models and product demand when you make a price change

- understanding how to assess competition and develop effective strategies to gain and protect your competitive advantage

- having the ability to understand your three basic financial statements - income statement; balance sheet, statement of cash flows

- being adept at delegating work and understanding people

- understanding business strategy and how to optimize and implement your short-term and long-term strategies

- understanding how to market your product/service using the 4P's and the promotional marketing mix

- optimizing value-added activities and minimizing non-value added activities within an organization by understanding the supply chain and the value chain

- understanding fundamentals of cutting edge process improvement methodologies such as Lean Six Sigma

Well, that might seem a bit daunting! What I am about to show you is a distillation of the core elements that *I consider* to be the most useful from my business studies and from my personal experiences. As an analogy, think sifted gold! Spending the time learning the materials that I am about to present will help you to more effectively and efficiently run your business and could very well *give you the upper hand over the competition.* These primers will *specifically* cover the following topics:

- a basic understanding of marketing

- a basic understanding of accounting

- a basic understanding of economics

- a basic understanding distribution channels

- a basic understanding of strategy

- learning how to make justified decisions

- realizing that you can't do it all – team building

- basic project management skills

- filtering and testing your entrepreneurial ideas

Before you delve into these primers, I would like to conduct an experiment. I mentioned in the Introduction that it was a myth that you needed to be born with certain attributes in order to be an effective entrepreneur. After you finish this section, I want you to think about how you feel about this myth before these primers and then after. Now, roll up your sleeves, were going in....

Part I
Basic Accounting

"It sounds extraordinary, but it's a fact that balance sheets can make fascinating reading"

Mary Lady Archer

Before we begin I need to give you the "big picture" on accounting. Years of commitment are required on behalf of professional accountants to grasp and to properly apply the subtle nuances of the accounting rules. Therefore, it is important to realize that this primer is not intended as a substitute for the professional accounting requirements of any business. The point of this primer and the value that it brings is the bridging of fundamental knowledge gaps that will possibly exist between you and your accountant. It is my intention to make your job and your accountant's job much easier by giving you the tools that will facilitate a more productive discourse between the two of you. It will also provide you with an excellent opportunity to truly understand your businesses finances and to save you considerable amounts of money by taking some of the work away from your accountant.

Before we begin I need to give you a quick warning: of the following primers that you are about to undertake, accounting will probably be the most tedious, so please do not feel discouraged if you need to take it slowly. The reward for your persistence will be realized in spades. The payoff? Well, once you grasp the basic concepts of accounting, you will be able to plan your business more effectively and better understand the health of it as you monitor its progression over time. It is well worth the effort. Even though this primer is presented at a less rigorous level than professional accounting, it will make you conversant with the vernacular of accounting and bookkeeping. In short, your accountant will love you! If certain concepts seem too hard to grasp or my descriptions just don't hit home, I encourage you to consult other sources such as the *accounting coach.com*.

Depending on where you live, you should realize that accounting principles vary from country to country. However, what I am about to show you should be reasonably close to what you will see in the Americas, UK and Europe. As with any accounting rules, it is fundamental and universal that all accounting entries be *relevant and reliable*; keep this top of mind as we proceed.

Basic Accounting Principles and Definitions

To understand what to do when you encounter the inevitable accounting-related "forks in the road" (believe me, at times it seems that *nothing* is clear cut in accounting) you will need to refer to the following definitions to help guide you through. These definitions may seem somewhat abstract, but they are very important. They are as fundamental to accounting as anatomy is to doctors and equations are to engineers.

Definitions:

Account – An account is a record of activities

Accruals concept – revenues and costs are recognized in the accounts when incurred or earned – *not* necessarily when money is received or paid

Accrual Accounting – Accrual accounting refers to the accumulation of payables on purchases (what you owe for items that you have purchased from someone) and receivables on sales (what you are owed for items that someone else purchased from you)

General Ledger – The general ledger account includes all asset accounts and liability accounts associated with the business. Examples of asset accounts include: cash account, inventory account and accounts receivable. Examples of liability accounts include: accrued expenses payable, notes payable and accounts payable. All of the information contained in the general ledger account is used to create financial statements, which are: the Balance Sheet, Income Statement (or Profit & Loss - P&L Statement) and Statement of Cash Flows

Double Entry Accounting – This is the process of entering a credit or debit into two separate accounts for every transaction. Credits and debits must be equal and balance every transaction

T-Account – A T-Account is given its name based on its appearance and function. It appears on a page as a large "T". The T-Account is an informal term that describes a set of records (e.g. revenue account, accounts payable, accounts receivable) that use double-entry accounting. Debits and credits are entered into each of the T-accounts

Principles:

Revenue Recognition Principle – A fundamental aspect of accrual accounting; it is the process of recording revenues as they are earned (product shipped, services rendered). Revenue is recognized typically when you ship your product, not when you actually get paid – a very important distinction. This does not preclude the possibility of rendering services/shipping product and receiving payment simultaneously – typical of a cash only business

Matching Principle – This is the requirement that a company matches expenses with related revenues in the time that they occur

Regularity Principle – This principle stipulates that a firm must adhere to the accounting rules and laws of your country/jurisdiction

Principle of Prudence – This principle addresses unethical, possibly illegal practices of deliberately exploiting areas of accounting and making accounts appear better than they actually are. Sometimes referred to as "window dressing", the result is to give the false impression that the business is performing better than it actually is. This principle states that one should not engage in dubious accounting activities and ensure that accounts are not misleading in any way. The *exact* amount of revenue, no more, no less must be entered when it is reasonably certain that the expense is receivable. Expenses must be fully recorded when they are incurred. This is somewhat related to the principle of conservatism, which is defined next

Principle of Conservatism – This principle states that when doubt exists between two acceptable alternatives then the accountant must choose the alternative that yields the lesser amount of profit, asset value or overall benefit

Principle of Periodicity – This principle states that an account entry must be made in the period that it occurred. If payment for a service, such as an insurance policy, is made as a lump sum then that lump sum should be broken up and entered evenly into the period that the service covers. An example might be a 1 year term insurance policy that was paid fully on January 1 but is "consumed" and then expensed equally over the following 12 months

Principle of Materiality/Full Disclosure – States that all relevant financial information pertaining to the business must be disclosed

Principle of Consistency – States that the methodology for treating accounts and entering transactions will be done in an unbiased, consistent manner

Definitions done! If some of these definitions or principles are about as clear as mud to you, please don't be discouraged. That is completely understandable because they have been presented to you out of context. For now, just read on and I think that the mud will begin to dissipate to a dense fog…….next an annoying haze……..and finally clarity! Hey, no one said it was going to be easy. Later on, come back and quickly re-read the definitions and I am sure that they will make more sense after you have seen them used in context.

Now let's begin by briefly discussing cash-only businesses. Businesses that deal exclusively as cash-only are businesses that, as the name implies, don't take or give credit and transact specifically with cash. In the mainstream world of accounting, cash-only businesses are much less common than companies using accrual methods, so it is somewhat unlikely that the business that you start will end up being a cash-only venture. So, for the rest of us mortals, the vast majority who do not deal with cash-only businesses, we will need to become familiar with the principles of accrual accounting.

Accrual accounting involves the process of recording non-cash sales as revenue - also called *accrued sales*, which is like an IOU *from* a customer after you have rendered services or have shipped products to them. The next step is balancing the revenue account entry with an entry for the same amount into accounts receivable.

Similarly, when an expense is incurred (i.e. you bought supplies) the transaction is entered into your accounts payable and balanced by an entry into your inventory account even though no cash has actually changed hands.....yet. You received goods and now you owe your supplier money. Eventually cash will change hands; however this typically happens at about 30 to 60 days after the sale. A key point to accrual accounting is that transactions should be matched. As you read in the Definitions, the matching principle states that expenses should be matched to related revenues in the time that they occur. Note that if this cause and effect relationship between expenses and revenues cannot be established (for example, R&D expenses or perhaps advertising expenses, where resulting revenues are very hard to attribute to what was spent) then the expense is recorded immediately in the month it was incurred, and is not accrued. The advantage of matching expenses and revenues is that you can gauge the profitability of those specific expenditures (ignoring R&D, advertising etc.) at any time.

So what are the advantages of accruals? *First*, most customers prefer credit – and you have to give the customer what they want. *Second, you* are going to want credit. To reduce the problems related to low cash inflows (due to unpaid receivables from your customers) you will *want* credit from your suppliers. In other words, you don't get paid for thirty days, *but* you don't have to pay for thirty days, which keeps your cash account reasonably neutral.

Earlier I mentioned the process of entering two inputs for every transaction, which is known as double entry accounting. Double entry accounting is based on the premise that for every transaction, there will be two balancing and equal entries that are actually inputted as *"debits"* and *"credits"*. Now, from my experience, debits and credits can *seem* mind bogglingly confusing, but they don't have to be. It is merely an accounting convention, and you just have to accept it and go with it – as opposed to trying to reason why.

OK, double entry accounting; what are the advantages?

- two entries track exactly where the money is going – VERY important

- the system is <u>self-checking</u> because the debits that are entered must equal the credits and this makes it very hard to make a mistake

Those are some very powerful checks and balances!

So how are debits and credits actually used? A transaction is either a debit or a credit depending on the type of account that is being debited or credited. Here are the distinctions:

Asset and Expense Accounts: debit to increase the account, credit to decrease the account

Liability, Equity & Income Accounts: credit to increase, debit to decrease

To clarify, I will introduce "T accounts" to help you wrap your head around this and to memorize it.

Aside: I know this may seem like your waist deep in it now, but please stay with me. Pretty soon that light bulb above your head will begin to glow and you will be glad that you put the effort in. Best of all, once you understand what is happening, you won't even need to deal with it on such a basic level because your accounting software will automatically take care of this dirty work for you. It is <u>critical,</u> however that you understand what is happening under the hood of your software and don't treat it like a black box.

T accounts

T-accounts are where the proverbial rubber meets the road. This is your interface between your business activities and your calculated financial statements. To begin, please study the following diagram:

<u>Double Entry Accounting</u>

Balance Sheet Accounts		
ASSET	**LIABILITY**	**EQUITY**
debit	debit	debit
(increase)	(decrease)	(decrease)
credit	credit	credit
(decrease)	(increase)	(increase)

Income Statement (or P&L) Accounts	
EXPENSE	**REVENUE**
debit	debit
(increase)	(decrease)
credit	credit
(decrease)	(decrease)

T-Accounts and Double Entry Accounting

The first thing that I have to say is that the above diagram is for reference only because your accounting software package, for example QuickBooks, is going to handle the double entry aspect on its own. It does, however, behoove you to understand it. I haven't yet addressed the Balance Sheet or the Income Statement so you will want to pop back here after I do to really get the full picture. For now, understand that if your debits don't equal your credits, then your balance sheet will not balance = BAD!! Now let's work our way through an example that should help to clarify.

Let's suppose that you sell an item for $1000 and you invoice your customer for this amount. You have earned revenue and therefore want to *increase* the *revenue account* by $1000. Referencing the above chart we can see that if we want to increase the *revenue account*, we need to "credit" it ($1000). Next, there needs to be a balancing entry. As we have learned already from accrual accounting, we have not received cash for the sale and are owed the $1000 by the customer. To formalize this situation, we need to first understand that someone owing us money is an asset – specifically it's a *receivable* and must be entered into *accounts receivable*. If you refer to the above chart, you will see that for an asset to be increased you need to "debit" it. You debit *accounts receivable* by $1000. Entry is now complete and balanced.

Fast forward to when the customer actually pays the invoice. You receive cash, deposit it into the bank and then account for it by increasing your *cash account* (an asset account) by $1000. Looking at the chart, you can see that increasing an asset account requires a *debit* (of $1000). Now, as per double entry accounting requirements, we need to balance this input. Since we are no longer owed the money from the customer, the *accounts receivable* must be reduced, and to decrease it we need to credit it $1000. OK, that's the cycle for a sale and payment. You can extrapolate this information for other scenarios. Best of all, when you go through the documentation for your specific accounting software it will become much clearer. Ok, now let's move onto financial reporting, beginning with the Income Statement.

The Profit and Loss Statement or Income Statement

As you read this section, please refer to the P&L template listed below. The first step to understanding this statement is to understand the top line, which is revenue. Revenue is simply your sales for a given period; typically a month, quarter or year.

The next series of lines show how the Costs of Goods Sold (COGS) is calculated. If you look closely at the P&L template, you will see the following equation is actually part of the statement. Compare the two to make sure that you understand that they are indeed the same.

- **COGS = Opening Inventory (at your cost) + Purchases (at your cost) – Closing Inventory (at your cost)**

Note, "*at your cost*" simply refers to the amount that you paid for materials or inventory.

So, by knowing how to calculate the COGS, we are now in a position to understand the major components of the Profit and Loss (P & L) or Income Statement as shown below:

P&L or Income Statement Template

Revenues		A
Opening inventory	b	
+ Purchases	c	
- Closing inventory	d	
Cost of Service/Cost of Goods Sold		b + c - d
Gross Profit [Revenue – COGS]		A – [b + c - d]
less **Operating Costs**		
Administrative expenses	e	
Rent	f	
Distribution costs	g	
Overheads	h	
Depreciation	i	[e + f + g +h + i]
Operating Profit		Gross profit - [e + f + g +h + i]
less Interest expense	j	j
Profit before tax		Operating Profit - j
less taxes	k	k
Profit for financial period		Profit before tax – k
less Dividends	l	l
Retained Earnings		Profit for financial period – l

Using the above template, I will create an Income Statement for the following example. You can refer to the completed template below to follow along with the example. Suppose that we have an entrepreneur named Jane. Jane founded and operates a shoe company in which she purchases shoes from manufactures and then sells them to the public at a mark-up or margin. Our first step will be figuring out the COGS. Let's say that her starting inventory on January 1 is $20,000 which was at her cost. In January, she orders and receives $100,000 (her cost) of shoes. In January, she sells $150,000 (includes her costs + markup); which is also known as Revenue for the month. Finally, her closing inventory on January 31 is $30,000 (at her cost). Neglecting freight, we have enough information here to calculate the COGS:

- **COGS = Opening Inventory + Purchases − Closing Inventory**

COGS = $20,000 + $100,000 − $30,000 = $90,000

With the COGS calculated, we are away to the races now! Since we know the revenues for the month ($150,000) and the COGS, we can calculate the Gross Profit. As you can see on the P&L Template, the COGS is subtracted from the Revenues which leaves us with the Gross Profit:

- **Gross Profit = Revenues - COGS**

Gross Profit = $150,000 − $90,000 = $60,000

Next, we can work our way down the template and calculate

the Gross Profit Margin or Gross Margin for short (note: whenever you see the word "margin", think "%"):

- **Gross Margin = Gross Profit/Revenue X 100%**

Gross Margin = $60,000/$150,000 x 100% = 40%

Now, suppose that Operating Expenses or "OPEX" for short (wages, general and administrative expenses, insurance, rent, depreciation) for the month of January totals $10,000, we can now calculate the Operating Profit:

- **Operating Profit = Gross Profit – Operating Costs**

Operating Profit = $60,000 - $10,000 = $50,000

Operating Profit Margin is (again, think "%" when you see the word margin):

- **Operating Profit Margin = Operating Profit/Revenues X 100%**

Operating Profit Margin = $50,000/$150,000 X 100% = 33.3%

STOP! Look back to see how far you have come! You are almost finished learning the Income Statement. You should be very proud of your efforts so far. Go, make a coffee or tea and relax for a while. You've earned it!

Depreciation: You may have noticed that I just kind of threw in the depreciation of equipment into the operating expenses without explanation. If you have heard of depreciation before, you may associate it with a loss in value of a physical asset (e.g. "my car depreciated by $5,000 as soon as I drove it off the lot"). Fixed assets, such as equipment are treated in an interesting way by accountants and the notion of loss in value is not the whole story. So, here is how depreciation really works.

Suppose that Jane pays $50,000 cash for a piece of equipment. You might expect that her accountant would simply enter the entire $50,000 that was paid for the asset into her income statement as an expense during the month that the asset was purchased. By now I'm pretty sure that you won't be surprised when I tell you that it's not that simple. Instead of putting in an entry for the total amount paid for that asset in the month that it was acquired, her accountant will enter a *fraction* of the total amount paid for the asset into *each of the coming months until the asset is deemed obsolete (defined in the accounting standards for your country)*. The accountant will subtract each of these fractions paid from the original cost of the asset until eventually the "salvage or scrap value" (*i.e. the final value at the end of its useful life*) has been achieved. So the portion that is expensed is a fraction of the asset *cost* which ideally should parallel the loss in value of that asset that occurs over time. Sounds confusing, I know, so to clarify the depreciation process, let's use some real numbers. Imagine that Jane's asset has an expected life span of five years before it is considered obsolete and therefore reaches its scrap value or salvage value of $5,000 at 60 months. The amount to be expensed over the five years is the *"original value minus the scrap value"*, which is $45,000. If the amount that was paid is spread out equally and expensed over the five year period, then the yearly depreciation charge on the income statement (operating expenses account) is $9,000 for each of the next five years or $750 per month (based on "straight line" depreciation method). The following chart should help to clarify further.

Depreciation Calculator	Undepreciated Asset Cost	Annual Depreciation	Total Monthly Depreciation Expense
Straight-line depreciation over 5 years Scrap value = 5000 Assume asset lifespan = 5 years			
Starting values for Year 1 and depreciation amounts	$ 50,000	$ 9,000	$ 750
Year 1 end	$ 41,000	$ 9,000	$ 750
Year 2 end	$ 32,000	$ 9,000	$ 750
Year 3 end	$ 23,000	$ 9,000	$ 750
Year 4 end	$ 14,000	$ 9,000	$ 750
Year 5 end	$ 5,000	$ 9,000	$ 750

Depreciation Calculation

Again, this particular method of spreading out the expense equally over five years is known as *straight-line depreciation* method. There are other methods (declining balance, double-declining balance, asset activity, units of time, units of production) that may for example, depreciate the asset much faster at the beginning its lifespan and less during the end. Different depreciation approaches may offer certain tax advantages over others. Choosing the ideal approach; one that optimizes your particular situation, falls within the purview of your accountant. Also, your country's federal or state/provincial governments may have very specific rules that dictate what approaches are permitted. One final word on depreciation; even though it is a line item on both the balance sheet and the income statement, *it's not an actual cash flow*. When you purchase equipment, you will have to pay the piper for the full amount before you receive that asset; that's when the cash truly *flows*! So depreciation is an income statement and balance sheet entry; *not an actual monthly cash payment* and as with any expense, it is subtracted from gross profits. We haven't yet discussed the balance sheet; however, I should say that the assets and depreciation, as they are shown on the Balance sheet are presented differently than on the P&L statement. On a Balance Sheet, the asset that was purchased has its *current residual value* (its approximate value *at that time*) listed and the accumulated depreciation to date; both seen on the Depreciation Calculation spreadsheet.

Ok, Depreciation is done and now back to our P&L statement.

Now that we are finished with operating profit margin, the next deductions on the income statement are interest and taxes.

Interest: Equipment, such as the machine that Jane purchased had to be fully paid for before she could officially take possession of it. The money that was used to pay for the equipment had to come from either her Cash Account or from a loan. Alternatively, she could have worked with a leasing company, however for start-ups, leasing can be quite an expensive option - if it is an option at all. Remember that start-ups typically are viewed as high risk and few lessors want to be involved with high risk customers. For that reason, let's neglect the leasing option. With regard to Jane's purchase, let's change the scenario and assume that Jane chose to finance the purchase instead of using cash. A good reason for this strategy might be to protect her operating capital that is needed to cover operating expenses, not buying fixed assets.

For this example, assume that Jane could get an attractive interest rate of 5% from the lender, contingent on her paying 20% or $10,000 down in cash for the $50,000 item - and financing 80% or $40,000. So, to see what Jane's monthly obligation is for a $40,000 loan, we need to generate an amortization schedule. Using an amortization schedule template in Open Office (LOVE this FREE software!) or Excel, with an assumed interest rate of 5%, amortized over a period of 5 years, the following schedule is created.

Amortization Schedule Calculator for OpenOffice
For any suggestion or feedback visit www.amortization-schedule.info website.

loan amount:	40000			
interest rate:	5.00		periodic payment:	754.85
loan length:	5		number of	
pay periodicity:	12		payments:	60

PERIOD:	INTEREST:	PRINCIPAL:	REMAINING:
0			40000
1	166.67	588.18	39411.82
2	164.22	590.63	38821.19
3	161.75	593.10	38228.09
4	159.28	595.57	37632.52
5	156.80	598.05	37034.47
6	154.31	600.54	36433.93
7	151.81	603.04	35830.89
8	149.30	605.55	35225.34
9	146.77	608.08	34617.26
10	144.24	610.61	34006.65
11	141.69	613.16	33393.49
12	139.14	615.71	32777.78
13	136.57	618.28	32159.50
14	134.00	620.85	31538.65
15	131.41	623.44	30915.21
16	128.81	626.04	30289.17
17	126.20	628.65	29660.52
18	123.59	631.26	29029.26
19	120.96	633.89	28395.37
20	118.31	636.54	27758.83
21	115.66	639.19	27119.64
22	113.00	641.85	26477.79
23	110.32	644.53	25833.26
24	107.64	647.21	25186.05
25	104.94	649.91	24536.14
26	102.23	652.62	23883.52
27	99.51	655.34	23228.18
28	96.78	658.07	22570.11
29	94.04	660.81	21909.30
30	91.29	663.56	21245.74
31	88.52	666.33	20579.41
32	85.75	669.10	19910.31
33	82.96	671.89	19238.42
34	80.16	674.69	18563.73
35	77.35	677.50	17886.23
36	74.53	680.32	17205.91
37	71.69	683.16	16522.75
38	68.84	686.01	15836.74
39	65.99	688.86	15147.88
40	63.12	691.73	14456.15
41	60.23	694.62	13761.53
42	57.34	697.51	13064.02
43	54.43	700.42	12363.60
44	51.52	703.33	11660.27
45	48.58	706.27	10954.00
46	45.64	709.21	10244.79
47	42.69	712.16	9532.63
48	39.72	715.13	8817.50
49	36.74	718.11	8099.39
50	33.75	721.10	7378.29
51	30.74	724.11	6654.18
52	27.73	727.12	5927.06
53	24.70	730.15	5196.91
54	21.65	733.20	4463.71
55	18.60	736.25	3727.46
56	15.53	739.32	2988.14
57	12.45	742.40	2245.74
58	9.36	745.49	1500.25
59	6.25	748.60	751.65
60	3.13	751.65	0.00

Amortization schedule

From the above amortization schedule, you can see that Jane will have a monthly obligation of $754.85 and a total commitment of $5,290.96 in interest before the loan is repaid.

Also, note from the first line of the schedule, which is January; she has an interest obligation of $166.67 for that month. So, $754.85 is entered into the January Income Statement, and unlike the depreciation expense, this payment is a real cash expense; she actually has to write a cheque to the bank.

Taxation

Taxation is an unavoidable expense for all *profitable* businesses. For this discussion, we will assume that Jane's business is structured as a corporation, a legal entity unto itself, like a natural person, completely distinct from Jane and her personal assets. Depending on your local tax laws, incorporating generally has the downside of double taxation. Double taxation means that the corporation must remit taxes on earnings and then from the net profit, you are paid a dividend (if the director(s) elect to pay one) and the n you must pay taxes on the monies that you receive from the corporation. Note, if you are an owner/operator your salary would be paid to you from *operating costs* (i.e. pre-corporate tax dollars) and is not subject to double taxation, but is subject to potentially very high personal income tax rates (over 50%!!!) if you are paid a high income. Also, note that dividends may be taxed at different rates than your salary depending on the tax laws of your country. Despite double taxation, there is still significant upside to incorporating your business. I have been driving this point relentlessly, but it's definitely worth mentioning again. Incorporation can mean not losing everything that you own if things should really go wrong (read this: lawsuits!) Note: if you provide _personal_ _guarantees_ on loans or other encumbrances, then the corporate structure will very likely *not* shield you from these liabilities. Be very careful with personal guarantees! Also, if you commit fraud or various other illicit acts, forget it; the corporate shield will not help you.

Now back to Jane. Looking at an example of corporate taxation, let us assume that Jane's corporate tax rate is 12%. So, once interest and depreciation charges have been accounted for, then taxes on profits are payable on the remaining balance. As you will see in the completed Income Statement below, Jane's Snazzy Sneakers must remit $5980 in corporate taxes for January's activities. Often this is required quarterly but it depends on your jurisdiction. As an aside, if Jane had structured as a sole proprietor, her tax situation *may* have been better, but the downside risk associated with this structure may far outweigh any potential tax advantages. Being structured as a sole proprietor could expose her personal assets. I know, I know, "who sues shoes stores!?" You might be surprised; law suits have a way of popping out of the ether, so please think carefully about your exposure. As far as taxes are concerned, speak to your accountant/lawyer about the relative advantages and disadvantages of incorporation vs. sole proprietorships.

Dividends

After the company has covered its tax liability, the balance of the profit is either streamed towards payouts in the form of dividends or kept within the company as retained earnings. In Jane's case, as the sole owner of the company, she decides not to take a dividend and chooses to leave the entire net profit within the company as retained earnings. These retained earnings are entered into the balance sheet and have the effect of increasing the retained earnings already on the balance sheet from the last accounting period. Note that the amount shown for the retained earnings in the Balance Sheet is the sum of all retained earnings since the inception of the company. Below is the final Income Statement for Jane's company in January. If the company had had a net loss for the year, then the Total Equity Balance in the balance sheet would decrease from the last accounting period to reflect this.

Income Statement: Jane's Snazzy Sneakers
January 2012
($000's)

Revenue		150
Opening inventory	20	
+ Purchases	100	
- Closing inventory	30	
Cost of Service/Cost of Goods Sold		(90)
Gross Profit [Revenue – COGS]		60
less **Operating Costs**		
Administrative expenses	4	
Rent	2.25	
Distribution costs	1	
Overheads	2	
Depreciation	0.75	10
Operating Profit		50
less Interest expense	0.166	0.166
Profit Before Tax		49.833
less taxation	5.98	5.98
Profit for financial period		43.85
less Dividends	0	0
Retained Earnings		43.85

The Balance Sheet

Where the P & L statement shows how the company has performed during a selected accounting period (in our example, one month), the balance sheet provides a snapshot of the company's assets, liabilities and owners' equity at any given point in time. Before delving into the specifics of the balance sheet, we need to first understand the accounting equation, because the balance sheet is based on this equation.

- **Assets − Liabilities = Equity**

Or re-written as:

- **Assets = Liabilities + Equity**

I have to admit that I used to really struggle with the accounting equation until I realized that Equity is effectively a loan to the company from shareholders (e.g. paid in capital) and therefore the company is on the hook for this money, just as it is on the hook for the Liabilities in the accounting equation. Combining the Equity portion with Liabilities to get Overall Liabilities - although not a convention used by accountants - helps me to wrap my head around the equation. When you think of it this way then the accounting equation says:

- **Assets = Overall Liabilities**

Anyway, with that said, back to the Balance Sheet.

The accounting equation simply states that the difference between what a company owns and what it owes defines the equity the shareholders hold in the company; what the company owes to the shareholders. A simple analogy would be taking the market value of your home and subtracting the balance of your mortgage which would yield the equity that you hold; what the "house owes you" if you sold it. The balance sheet utilizes this equation, addressing all assets and liabilities, current, mid-term and long-term. Before applying information from Jane's Snazzy Sneaker Company to a balance sheet, we will look at a balance sheet template first. Now in case I have confused you on this point, a "current" asset is an asset that is cash or cash-like (easily converted to cash, like finished goods). Current assets are near cash holdings. "Current" liabilities refer to short-term encumbrances that are due very soon, such as the next 30 to 60 days.

Balance Sheet Template

Balance Sheet: Company Name

Period Ending	December 31 2011	December 31 2010
Assets:		
Cash and Cash equivalents		
Short-term Investments		
Net Receivables		
Inventories		
Other Current Assets		
Total Current Assets:		
Long-term Investments		
Property, Plant & Equipment		
(less accumulated depreciation)		
Intangible Assets		
Total Assets:		
Liabilities:		
Current Liabilities		
Accounts Payable		
Short-term debt		
Other Current Liabilities		
Total Current Liabilities		
Medium and Long-term loans		
Total Liabilities		
Total Assets – Total Liabilities		
Shareholders Equity:		
Paid-in Capital		
Retained Earnings		

Using the balance sheet template, I will populate each line with information from Jane's Snazzy Sneakers financial information for fiscal years 2010 and 2011. What is important for you to understand is not just the actual numbers for each line, but the fact that the accounting equation is fundamental to balance sheet construction. That is, the sum of all retained earnings since the company started plus the paid in capital (i.e. total equity) is equal to the total assets minus the total liabilities. It is also very important to note the decreasing liquidity (i.e. ease of converting to cash) of assets as you move down the balance sheet from cash to intangible assets. Similarly, on the liability side as you go from the top (Accounts Payable) and move downwards to medium and long-term loans, the timeframe required for you to pay these liabilities increases. Note also, that balance sheets can be written either in stacked form as I have shown or in a split page format with the assets on the left and liabilities and equity on the right. Other than placement on the page, nothing else is different between the two formats. For the simplicity of it, I chose to show you the stacked version.

Balance Sheet: Jane's Snazzy Sneakers

Period Ending	December 31 2011	December 31 2010
Assets:	$(000's)	$(000's)
Cash and Cash equivalents	250	200
Short-term Investments	2	1
Net Receivables	30	22
Inventories (cost)	30	25
Other Current Assets	0	0
Total Current Assets:	**312**	**248**
Long-term Investments	5	3
Property, Plant & Equipment	300	250
(less accumulated depreciation)	(120)	(100)
Intangible Assets	0	0
Total Assets:	**497**	**401**
Liabilities:		
Current Liabilities		
Accounts Payable	10	8
Short-term debt	10	8
Other Current Liabilities	3	5
Total Current Liabilities	**23**	**21**
Medium and Long-term loans	80	30
Total Liabilities	103	51
Total Assets – Total Liabilities	**394**	**350**
Shareholders Equity:		
Paid-in Capital	50	50
Retained Earnings	344	300
Total Equity Capital	**394**	**350**

So, aside from the fact that the accounting equation is shown to hold true in the above example, it is also noteworthy that the total equity capital grew from year to year. Please remember that the balance sheet is merely a snapshot of what is owned, what is owed, what has been paid in (equity) plus what has been retained in total (equity).

So that wraps up our discussion of the balance sheet and the income statement. What I have shown you is quite basic, however, it is enough to allow you to work with small business bookkeeping software and to have a reasonable understanding of how to build and interpret these statements. As you become more comfortable with the software and reports that it can generate you can make a list of things of which you are unsure and run them by your accountant.

Statement of Cash Flows

With the P&L statement and the balance sheet under our belts, the next step *should* be to use the two statements to derive the statement of cash flows (SCF's) using "the indirect method" or the theoretically simpler, yet still daunting "direct method" – pretty advanced stuff I say. Notice that I said "*should* be", because the level of difficulty of constructing SCF's jumps up by orders of magnitude in comparison to the other statements. Therefore, I have chosen not to drag you through the minutia of these calculations. This is not to say that you don't need to understand the thought processes required for the construction of the statement, because that is important. Ultimately these statements created by your software will be vetted by your accountant, so a general understanding of the cash flow statement is more than enough.

So, what is a statement of cash flows? Well, it is a document that summarizes all of the ins and outs, literally, for the company cash account. The following is an example of a statement of cash flows (please notice the "+" and "-"signs as they indicate whether cash transactions add + or subtract − from the cash account)

Statement of Cash Flows

January 2011 to January 2012

Cash at beginning of year: _____

Operating Activities

+ Cash receipts from customers

+ Cash charges for depreciation

- Cash paid for leases

- Cash paid for rent

- Cash paid for salaries/hourly

- Cash paid for utilities

- Cash paid to suppliers

- Cash paid for maintenance

- Cash paid for logistics

Cash Flow from Operations

- Cash paid for interest

- Cash paid for dividends

- Cash paid for taxation

+ Cash received from loans

Total Cash Flow

As mentioned earlier, the statement of cash flows can be derived two ways:

1) The Direct Method

2) The Indirect Method

As implied by the name, the direct method refers to the creation of cash flow statement directly from the cash account transactions, sorting each transaction and then categorizing. Due to the meticulous detail required on the movement of cash and the sheer volume of cash transactions that most businesses experience, the impracticalities associated with this method make it less commonly used. Imagine having 20,000 separate cash receipts for the year and your cash balance and calculated balance disagree by $2.00….NOT fun, because you have to find out why it doesn't balance.

The indirect method is used much more frequently, and this is accomplished through the following steps:

1) Calculate the change in cash – This is done by simply comparing the cash accounts in the balance sheet between two different accounting periods. So as an example, for Jane's Snazzy Sneakers this means $250K - $200K = $50K cash growth.

2) Calculate the CFO – This is the difficult part (the one I didn't want to drag you through) that requires you to account for "noncash" transactions such as accrued accounts payable (the raw material inventory and work in progress (WIP) that you hold but technically don't own yet) and receivables (the cash flow that you weren't given yet but has already been stated in your revenues) and depreciation (writing down the expense of an asset that was, in reality paid for a long time ago; remember I said depreciation is a non-cash expense?).

So, in theory constructing cash flow statements "indirectly" *seems* pretty simple, however, in reality it takes some finesse, or sometimes, I swear a deal with the devil to get it right. I know, all of you folks with accounting backgrounds don't find it that difficult, but let's face it, you have had *a lot* practice, or in lieu of that – you made a deal with the devil.

It is very important to realize that cash truly *is* king and as a small business owner, the statement of cash flows is arguably the most important statement available to you. Being able to do the math to create this statement is, in my opinion, secondary to being able to interpret it. So, I suggest that you take the time to really understand this statement. Remember this rather obvious yet unsettling rule of thumb: *No cash = No business*. So, follow the money and always know where you stand.

There is one final caution with regard to cash flow projections. When you calculate your anticipated monthly expenses, realize that cash flow in and out of the business will not actually take place in nice tidy little packets each month like clockwork (like you probably have on your business plan). On the contrary, be prepared to take *huge* hits in your cash account when many expenses become payable at the same time *and* your debtors conveniently decide that they deserve an extra 30 days to pay you – or decide to not pay at all (delinquent accounts; bad debt). Account reconciliations will help but can't completely prevent you from going below zero $ in your cash account. To be absolutely sure that you don't accidently do this and then write NSF cheques, here is what you need to do: Arrange for a line of credit to help you to manage volatile spikes in cash demands that will surely happen. This line of credit that you set up will be in place to absorb these inevitable monetary shocks. You'll sleep better at night if you have it, guaranteed.

Financial Ratio Analysis

Another nice and tidy way to monitor the financial health of your business is to use ratio analysis. Ratio analysis gives you another way to interpret debt levels, cash levels, inventory levels as well as profitability at a glance. The data used to create ratios is extracted directly from the financial statements so the process can be easily automated. I won't be going through specific examples of calculating ratios because every industry has widely different ratio benchmarks and interpretations of these benchmarks. Finding these benchmarks and learning how to understand them is a key part of your due diligence. In this section, I will list the various ratios, the corresponding formulas and brief descriptions of each. However, I won't delve into a detailed discussion of each ratio. Now, please don't feel obliged to use all of the ratios that are listed here because there are many of them. When looking at ratios specific to your industry, make sure that you try your best to get comparables from many different sources. This may be very difficult if you are going into a very small or embryonic industry that doesn't typically publish financial information. In that case, you may have to be creative by searching similar industries within your market or in different geographical markets. Incumbents in distant markets who understand that you pose no competitive threat may be much more forthcoming. Also, search MBA thesis projects, government data, boards of trade, conventions, entrepreneurship clubs, economic development programs, internet communities, blogs and white papers.

Profitability ratios: The following ratios provide litmus tests for the profitability of your business.

- Gross profit margin (see Income statement)

- Operating profit margin (see Income statement)

- Return on investment (ROI) = net profit post tax and interest / shareholder's funds

- Return on capital = net profit / capital investment

- Return on net capital employed = net profit / net capital employed

- Dividend yield ratio = dividends paid out per share / value of stock per share

- Dividend payout ratio (payout ratio) = dividend per equity share / earnings per share

- Return on equity capital = (net profit post tax − dividend) / paid-in equity capital

- Earnings per share ratio = (net profit after interest, tax, dividends) / number of equity shares

Solvency Tests:

Solvency tests explore the company's ability to meet financial obligations; obviously very critical ratios.

- Current ratio = current assets / current liabilities

- Acid test ratio = current liquid assets / current liabilities

- Debt to equity ratio = (short term + long term debt) / total equity

We are now finished with ratios and financial reporting and will move on to the marketing primer – are you relieved? Note that we will delve into some management accounting later when we study Decision Making. Fear not, because management accounting is much more intuitive and even, dare I say....enjoyable. Onto Marketing!

Part II
Fundamentals of Marketing

"The aim of marketing is to know and understand the customer so well the product or service fits him and sells itself."
Peter F. Drucker

Now that you have a basic understanding of financial reporting, you are in a better position to tackle the marketing primer. The logical starting point for a primer on marketing should be to define what marketing actually means. From the literature, I sourced some pithy yet eloquent definitions:

"Marketing strategy is a response to <u>customer requirements</u>"
(Cohen, 2009)

"Marketing is the process of planning and executing the conception, pricing, promotion and distribution of ideas, goods, and services to create exchanges that <u>satisfy individual and</u>

organizational objectives"(Bennett, 1988)

"[Marketing is]...the process by which companies <u>create value</u> <u>for customers</u> and build strong customer relationships in order to capture value from customers in return" (Kotler, et.al. 2008)

The common thread amongst the three definitions (I took the liberty of underling in each definition) is _meeting customer requirements or needs_. This is very important and as I stated before, must be _the_ primary motivating factor for you offering your product or service.

Speaking of motivation, I realize that many people don't want to hear this, but you shouldn't be thinking about starting a business with a primary goal of "striking it rich". Because, _striking it rich_ clearly does not qualify as a "business idea" and provides a solution to no one's problems, _but your own_. Making money is one of many possible motivators to starting a business, but is definitely not reason enough to proceed. If a collective need has been addressed by your idea, money will flow. Therefore, you need to focus on how you can be the best person _anywhere_ to solve your customer's problems. Marketing is delivering that message.

Courses and textbooks on marketing often begin with an overarching perspective on the subject by looking at the various social trends that lead to new markets and eventually pull customers to purchase. Examples of such contemporary trends?

- the widespread adoption of the Internet-based commerce that has led to companies like Amazon or Ebay;

- the exponential growth in the use of social media sites;

- special demands stemming from the now ubiquitous (very conservatively 30%) one-parent families;

- the spawning of countless new markets stemming from the green movement and sustainability;

- the mass-adoption, integration and convergence of technologies (cameras, GPS, e-messaging, mp3, etc.) in smart phones

We will investigate these in greater depth later when we discuss finding market opportunities. In the interest of brevity, I have decided to fast-track to one of the core principles of marketing by focusing on a concept known as the *4 P's*. The 4 P's is a shorthand term for Product, Price, Promotion and Place. Let's investigate each of these in greater depth.

Product:

Finding and implementing solutions to problems, whether they are a physical product or a service, is the crux of your job as an entrepreneur. As mentioned before, your product may be a completely new innovation or it may simply be a much improved version of an old product. The Dyson Company has supremely marketed new renditions of old ideas: vacuum cleaners, hand dryers and fans. These are old products but with sexy new designs and approaches that *create and fulfill* customer needs. On the other end of the spectrum, all out innovation, which yields completely new and unique solutions to problems, such as the Internet, personal computer, microwave oven, fiber optics, transistor, internal combustion engine, pasteurization, radio and immunization are much harder to achieve. This is not to say that they are out of the realm of possibility - especially in the field of technology - they are just much more difficult to develop. Software development, often created on a very small scale, usually in garages for some strange reason, can yield spectacular results, such as DOS, Macintosh, iOS, Windows, Android, smart phone apps, YouTube, FACEBOOK, Amazon and Google. Notice that each of these innovations relied on pre-existing technological platforms or hierarchies. Hierarchy is critical, because it paves the way for technologies that were previously impossible or irrelevant. A good example of a hierarchy allowing for innovation is spreadsheet software. Excel's success was predicated on a technological and social paradigm shift: the introduction of the personal computer followed by mass adoption of the technology. Conversely, innovations may simply be "before their time". When the laser was invented it was dubbed, "*a solution looking for a problem*", akin to inventing Excel before PC's even existed. This phenomenon is summarized by Albert Einstein's statement: "*We can't solve problems by using the same kind of thinking we used when we created them*". For example, if we are looking for efficient ways to crunch huge numbers but still thinking *pencil and paper*, then Excel is not the logical result. However when thinking *personal computer,* then Excel is a very logical result. How irrelevant is the concept of a steam engine prior to the development of the metallurgy or the casting methods that would allow for adequate housing of high pressure steam? What good is an internal combustion engine without a reliable supply of liquid or gas hydrocarbon? How pointless is MRI, Radar, wireless communication and electronic digital storage without a power grid to support it? The point that I am driving at is that a breeding ground for entrepreneurial opportunity occurs where new technological paradigms are being rolled out. The shrewd entrepreneur keeps a jaundiced eye on new technology and should seek to find gaps of opportunity that exist as these technologies are being adopted. Being able to alter your perspective is the key to finding unique solutions and is the key to *lateral thinking*.

No matter what your product or service, you must bring *something* new to the table. This is product differentiation. If you fail to differentiate, you will be competing with the masses, who also haven't distinguished their product. In some respects, this will make your product commodity-like and could lead to potentially significant competition. It gets worse. Beyond being inundated with competitors, the nature of this competition will almost certainly tend towards the lowest common denominator; the most fundamental and cut-throat form of competition: *price-based competitiveness*. I have seen this before in the brewing industry, which is rife with imitation and duplication all under the guise of being "unique" or "artisan". Almost every microbrewery-made beer that you see says something to the effect of "small batches", "hand crafted", "choice hops and malt", "made by connoisseurs" and so on and so on. How can everyone be so "different" while delivering the same message? They can't. While so many of these breweries are busy pointing out how unique they are, the reality is that the only uniqueness that many of them have is their lock on a geographical area due to lack of competition. In short, their "strategic differential advantage" (we will discuss this term in more detail later) is that they have a *geographical* monopoly - as opposed to a technical or patent-related monopoly - in their immediate area or location. This is NOT a sustainable differential advantage and definitely not strategic. Inevitably, competitive forces in that geographical area will rise to the opportunity, and the brewery that once enjoyed the bliss and quiet life of a monopoly will see its status fade to duopoly, oligopoly and eventually to *perfect competition* (i.e. identical products, price takers, small market share, buyers know product/prices of all firms, easy entry/exit) where there is intense competition. Not good for long-term success, but great for customers as prices drop and *profits drop*. So, sustainability is the key; *fundamental* to your differential advantage. Choose the product/service that you can do better than anyone else – and do it sustainably. Want an example? This might seem to be way out of left field, but in my opinion it is a textbook example of a product, service or brand that is unique and very, *very* difficult to imitate. So what is it? It is the Howard Stern Show. Now that was a curve ball, wasn't it? OK, I promise I will try to make that my last baseball metaphor for this chapter. I bet I can guess what you are thinking right now; how can you possibly compare the Howard Stern Show with a small business start-up? Well, for one Howard Stern came from the humblest of beginnings and was originally a very small voice trying to compete *on the same grounds* as other disc jockeys. So what did he do? He changed the game. He realized that if he couldn't win with the "rules" written as they were, then he was going to change them, for everyone. He stopped trying to sound like the other DJ's and created his own sound, *his own brand* which centered around Howard just being himself, and as uncensored as possible; the first and the greatest "shock jock" to date. Now you may despise him, but you must give him credit for turning the status quo upside down by being completely unique, being branded the "King of all Media" and having the audacity to constantly challenge others to try to beat him. In response, many others do try to compete, and some do OK, such as Ron & Fez or Opie & Anthony on Sirius/XM. But in the big scheme of things, the vast majority of radio personalities simply don't have the ability to challenge his style, humor and approach. This is not just my opinion, the ratings support the argument. He is unique, he fulfills a need for millions, and so far, 30+ years later he can't be imitated, duplicated or beat. This is a prime example of *sustainable* differential advantage.

So, to summarize, when you are thinking of your product or service, think like Howard Stern, Henry Ford, Sir Richard

Branson and Steve Jobs/Steve Wozniak....BE UNIQUE! You don't need to create the next insulin (more power to you if you do though!) but do your best to find your own niche. Strive to be innovative, to be a first mover and be prepared to zig when the competition zags.

Price

Setting a price for your product/service that is considered fair to both you *and* your customers is a significant challenge but a critical one. What makes this so important is the fact that the effectiveness of your business model is very likely going to co-relate directly with how *well* you have priced it. Notice I didn't say how *low* you priced your product. If you set your prices too low then your margins will suffer and brand perception could suffer too. If you set your prices too high then sales will lag and your revenues will suffer. Therefore, you must strive to strike a balance between price points that are too high or too low by really nailing that sweet spot between the two extremes. During the due diligence phase of your planning, you should begin the pricing process by first estimating your optimum price point (more on how to do this later) and then estimating your anticipated monthly sales for the next three years based on that price point - *plus an annual incremental price increase equal to the inflation rate.* You can create rather sophisticated spreadsheets that co-relate a range of price points versus anticipated sales which will help you to find that sweet spot. Once you have settled on a price, the anticipated sales volumes need to be estimated.....three times: once for the very conservative sales projections, once for the most likely sales projections and once for the optimistic sales projections. Based on these sales projections, you will be creating pro-forma financial statements. Based on these financial statements, you will be undertaking a staggering array of tasks such as, securing (*and guaranteeing!*) banks loans, finding investor capital, committing to property leases and deciding upon the appropriate amount of equipment to be purchased, plus many, many others. Therefore, it behooves you to make your pricing as effective as possible. If your price point is sub-optimal, your revenues will not align with your projections and eventually you could fall short of cash. So, you must be reasonably sure about the marketplace acceptance of your pricing. So how is this done? Let's look at some of the methods that start-ups can use for setting prices for both innovative new offerings and for common products/services in mature markets.

Please remember this nice little rule of thumb for making any sale: *the price that you charge for your product or service must be less than or equal to the customer's perceived value.* To maximize your revenues you need to aim for "equal to" definitely NOT "less than"! So, if you optimally match your price with your customer's value perception, you will maximize revenues and therefore your profit too. The reverse is also true. If you don't optimize your pricing, then you will not optimize your profits; and may even be unprofitable. So, how do you get that "optimum" price? Looking at the following graph should convey the point:

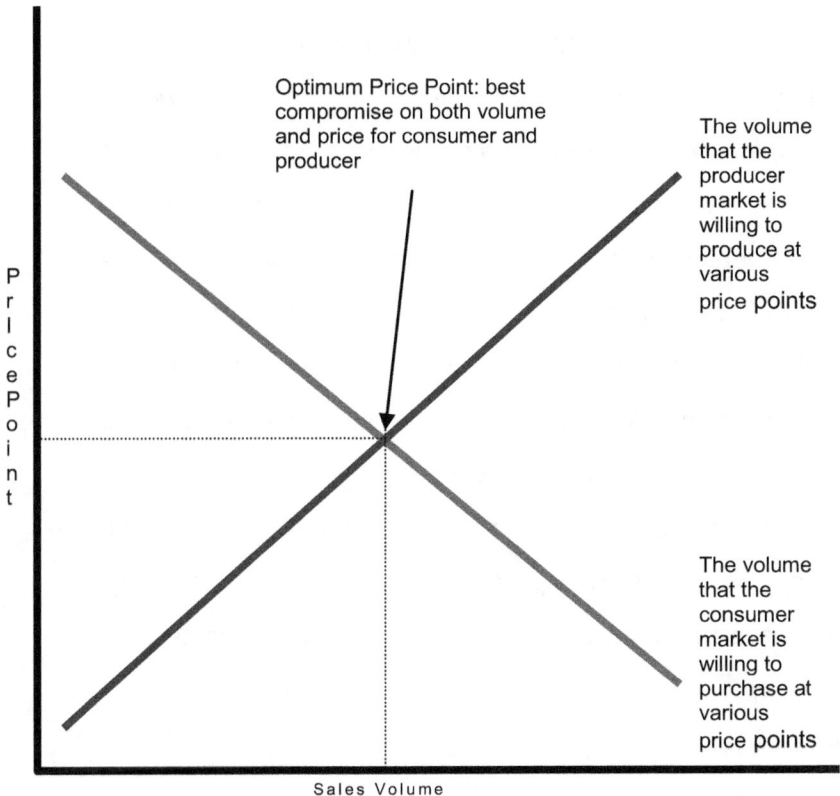

Price - Volume Relationship

The Price – Volume Relationship graph (also see Supply – Demand graph in the Economics section) shows the conflict that exists between the goals of consumer markets and the goals of producer markets. As we all know, rational consumers want to pay as little as possible for the products/services that they consume. Conversely, product producers want to receive as much as possible for their products; now that is conflict! This is exactly what each of the lines on the graph show and this is also why the slopes go the opposite way. From the graph, we can see that for the consumer market, as the price for a product drops, the tendency is to buy more and conversely for the producer market, as the price of the product drops the tendency is to produce less. The good news is that there is a compromise between the disparate goals of the consumer and producer: *optimum price point*. This is the point where the two graphs intersect. This point identifies a price point that is considered an equitable compromise for both of these markets; the only positive sum outcome available for both actually. Please keep this theory in mind as we proceed to investigate pricing approaches for two distinct types of products:

1) A new product/service that cannot be *directly* compared to any other product

2) A re-marketed product (like Dyson vacuums) that can be directly compared to another product — typically competing in a well-established, mature market.

Under scenario one, because of the ambiguous nature of the problem, the process of determining a price point presents a significant challenge. In the absence of direct price comparisons, there is no way to estimate accurately the market acceptance and subsequent demand for a unique product at various price points, so an element of trial and error is inevitable. The first step to arriving at an optimized price is to take all available knowledge of a chosen industry and combine it with any further research that can be done, such as, consumer surveys, test markets and focus groups. This information will allow you to make reasonable estimates for both pricing and for projected sales. Chicken and egg stuff I realize, but as common sense dictates, the more one knows about a market, the better the estimates will be.

Let's assume that you have fully explored your industry, perhaps you hired some college students to do a mini marketing study and you also spent a few thousand dollars on getting a focus group together. Through your efforts, you have established what you believe to be reasonable estimates for pricing and sales volumes for the "conservative", "most likely" and "optimistic" sales scenarios. Now, do yourself a *huge* favor and reduce your sales estimates by 10 - 25% (the more the better), for all three scenarios. I recommend this because you have very likely overestimated how many units you can actually sell, especially in the first year or two. Overestimating sales is common and is one of the ways that enthusiasm can actually work *against* you. Naturally you *really* want to see your venture get up and running, so on a subconscious level it is very easy to skew the numbers too optimistically. This mistake is typical of most entrepreneurs, seasoned or otherwise and is why I suggest that you soften your estimates a bit. These reductions, regardless of how painful they are to accept, will provide you with a hedge against the unknowns and unknowables associated with price setting. Now, revise all of your pro forma financial calculations based on the lowered estimates of sales and in the end use the conservative scenario for your price point and sales, not the optimistic or most likely. If your final estimates still show reasonable profit potential, you're definitely on the right track. If not, try to find legitimate savings in costs and then try again. If that doesn't work, you are faced with your first potential *"make you or break you"* decision as an entrepreneur. Please make the right one.

Speaking of costs, I want to give you a better understanding about how the different types of costs will vary as production output increases. The costs to which I refer are Cost of Goods Sold (COGS) and Operating Costs – our old friends from Accounting. For accuracy you should know that operating costs are the sum of your fixed operating costs plus your variable operating costs. As the names imply, fixed costs are stable and not volume dependent. Variable costs rise with increasing output. Generally speaking, as production output goes up and your business starts to produce substantial output, the COGS *per unit* may tend to drop because suppliers *may* offer price breaks at higher consumption levels. This is a part of something known as the *benefit of scale*. Now that I've given you that little nugget of information, I'm going to take it away from you. In the spirit of conservatism, I strongly suggest that you assume no benefit of scale price breaks from suppliers when doing your financial analyses. You do not want to rely on assumed volume-based price breaks that *may not* occur – doing so is the stuff of mavericks! There are relatively few reasons why price breaks may happen and conversely *a myriad* of reasons why they may not. For example, if there are only one or two suppliers ("concentrated suppliers") unless your purchases account for a major percentage of your supplier's sales, I can almost guarantee that you will *not* receive substantial price breaks. There is an even more worrisome scenario - that is, if you buy from an industry with few suppliers *and* you are a *very* small purchaser, as in *start-up*. Under this scenario, as a start-up you now have two strikes against you, and you should be prepared for price *increases*, not decreases. More will be discussed on the topic in the Strategy section when we discuss Supplier Power in Porter's Five Forces model. For now, don't bank on price breaks. Doing so is just too optimistic and you may never even make it to these greener pastures if you roll the dice and base your cash flow projections on overly optimistic scenarios. Despite your enthusiasm and hopes, be conservative!

Variable operating costs, such as hourly wages, will increase more or less in lock-step with production increases. Fixed operating costs, such as rent, salaries, insurance, lighting and heating costs, however, will stay roughly the same as production output goes up. Therefore, *on a per unit basis* fixed costs will trend downward with the increase in units produced. However, variable operating costs will stay constant on a per unit basis and COGS (ignoring benefit of scale) will also stay the same *on a per unit basis*. So, for example, if your fixed operating costs are $4000 per month and you made 4000 units, your fixed operating costs/unit is $1. However, if you double your output to 8000 units and, by definition, your total fixed operating costs don't change - you do not need more light or more rent to make more units - your fixed operating ***costs/unit*** drops to $0.50. This is why making more is a better thing.

OK, now that you understand why increased output is a good thing from a fixed cost perspective, let's apply this knowledge to a common real-world problem. Let's work through the process of setting a reasonable price point for a product that has no available comparisons. Let's assume, *based on the absolute minimum viable production level (i.e. maximum per unit costs)* that the COGS = $2.00 *per unit* and that the total operating costs = $1.00 *per unit* and therefore the COGS + operating costs = $3.00 *per unit*. To reiterate, these figures are based on the absolute minimum feasible output, which is the most costly per unit that can be produced – which is conservative. Let's also assume that at the minimum output, there is a debt service of $0.25/unit for equipment loans and therefore, we will need to amend the $3.00/unit figure upwards, *based on minimum demand/production levels,* to a total of $3.25 per unit. Since we are interested in making a profit, we cannot price the product at $3.25 because that would only break even at best. You need to add a reasonable operating profit that will make you happy and not make the final price tag unattractive to your customer. For our example, let's assume a profit of $1.00 and therefore a final price of $4.25. Utilizing this figure, let's apply some of our newfound accounting skills to calculate the gross profit, gross profit margin, operating profit and operating profit margin (please try this on your own before looking on – refer to P&L template in Accounting).

Gross Profit Calculation:

- **GP = Revenue – COGS**

GP = $4.25 – $2.00 = $2.25

GP margin = $2.25/$4.25 x 100%

GP margin = 52.94%

Operating Profit Calculation:

- **OP = GP – Operating Costs**

OP = $2.25 - $1.00 = $1.25

OP margin = $1.25/$4.25 x 100%

OP margin = 29.41%

The final price of $4.25 was built on the lowest possible output and therefore the absolute highest _per unit_ cost possible. This is good because it means that as volumes go up, then _per unit_ fixed costs have nowhere to go but down - guaranteed! This is not the same thing as price breaks from suppliers. As we discussed before, this is simply the result of a more efficient operation, churning out more units without the fixed portion of the operating costs going up. So, as volume increases, the operating profit margin will get higher and higher – up to a limit of course. This also means that the bottom line, net profits - i.e. profits after taxes, depreciation and interest - will also increase as volumes go up. Be aware that this favorable trend will continue right up until you *run out of physical space*. Running out of physical space is a much different problem then equipment related capacity limits. Production constraints caused from limitations in equipment capacity can be relatively easy to address with new equipment. Running out of physical space is a potential show stopper for a production facility and typically requires wholesale changes ($$) to the business. Think back to the case study and how the ownership structure of the company changed because of physical space needs. Running out of space means that you will need to accept one of the following scenarios:

- that you have reached your businesses maximum capable output and can no longer grow (revenues remain static)

- that you need to hire contractors to make any additional units (higher cost/unit)

- you need to expand your space to expand output capacity (higher cost/unit initially)

- you need to move to a bigger facility to expand output capacity (higher cost/unit initially)

Not great options, but if you have maxed out you plant's capacity *and you are profitable*; you have done well. Conversely, if you have maxed out your plant's capacity and you are not profitable, then you have a big decision to make. Let's assume the former, that you are profitable. If this were to be the case then the odds would be good that your current account and your borrowing capacity would be healthy enough to take on an expansion. The moral of this story is, if you hit this milestone and if you do decide to expand, your profitability is going to go down, either permanently or temporarily. Either way, it is going down. Make sure that you have the provisions in place to endure the costs of a mass expansion AND reduced margins at the same time. Now here is the good news. As your volumes increase beyond your previous highs, your product's profitability will trend back to where it was and could eventually get to a higher level than it was before the expansion.

So as you can see, once all of the anticipated costs have been incorporated, the analysis of establishing a price point gets to be much more interesting and its implications far reaching. In the end, I strongly recommend that you go with the conservative scenario for planning your business. It is your safest bet because of the hedge it provides against the possibility of poor sales estimates. Also, please don't feel that taking the time to calculate the *most likely* and the *optimistic* scenarios is wasted because they're not necessarily throwaways. If your sales end up outperforming your conservative scenarios and trend closer to either the most likely or to the optimistic scenarios, you can use those calculations and pro-forma estimates as a guide instead. Frankly, it is a good problem to have. Now, that's the difference between a maverick and an entrepreneur.

Now that we have looked at a quantitative approach to establishing your price point within an ambiguous business environment, it is time to explore a pricing strategy when much more information is at hand. What if you are considering entrance into a market that is fairly well established? The fact is that the task of establishing price points will be much easier if you are entering an existing market. The obvious downside, of course, is that where comparables exist, so too does competition. If baseline prices for your industry are already in place then you have a reasonable and much less risky starting point for your pricing. Let's explore an example for setting pricing under this scenario.

Suppose you are considering starting up a new lawn care service; however, there are already numerous other lawn care companies in your area. You know that the competition charges on average $50 per grass cutting based on a "twenty visits per season" commitment by a client. Additionally, all of these competitors include three chemical based weed-n-feed treatments as part of their service. You have studied the market and believe that the only differentiation that you can see between each of these competitors is related to their customer service. You have identified significant variation in the quality of service between companies, specifically with promptness, reliability, professionalism and thoroughness. You believe that you can easily and significantly beat the competition on each of these accounts. In addition to this, you have *specialized knowledge* of organic lawn-care chemistry and soil chemistry. You have observed major societal trends towards green living, and to profit from those trends you have developed a proprietary *organic* weed treatment that contains ingredients that cannot harm the environment, people or animals. With this knowledge, you believe that you can strategically and sustainably differentiate your services from your competitors. *Strategically*, because you are introducing a safer approach to the lawn-care business with a *first mover advantage*, which is being the first and only company around that can offer a harmless organic substance to eliminate weeds. Sustainably, because you had the foresight to patent protect your formula. With this sustainable differential advantage, you believe that you can justify a premium for your service. You *believe* that the environmentally and safety conscious customer will gladly pay a premium for your product because you <u>have solved a perceived problem</u> for them. Based on this, when doing your financial analyses you might want to experiment with a higher, say 10-20%, price point at $60 - $65 per visit. Being sustainably unique in the market affords you the luxury of charging a premium for your service - which ties into our "Price-Volume" discussion from before. With regard to your costs, if they cannot be aligned with price to yield a reasonable profit, you will probably need to find new sources for raw materials or you will need to experiment with higher price points – to a reasonable limit. What it boils down to is how much more - or less - do the raw materials cost in comparison to traditional chemical-based treatments. If costs are the same or less, then your business model is clearly superior to your competitions. If you market your services as well as, or even better than, the competition, your business should make serious inroads in the marketplace.

OK, so what was the point of this example? Well, actually there are a three. The first point is to realize that having established industry prices takes much of the guess work out of the pricing challenge. The second point is to realize that any *sustainably* unique quality that your product possesses over the competition may justify a price premium. Notice that I said *may* justify, which leads me to my third point. Business models based on intuition as opposed to hard data are potential red herrings and intrinsically risky. In this case, beyond reasonable speculation on market trends for sustainable organic solutions, there is no *definitive* proof that customers will actually want it. Despite the promising nature of this product, it is a prime example of a business idea that needs to be supported by some market feedback *before* proceeding. If that seems too onerous, look at it this way. If you were to approach some sort of sophisticated investor such as an angel or venture capitalist, about backing you on this project, I can assure you that they would demand *conclusive and unbiased* market research indicating an unequivocal need for your product relative to the competition. So, I ask you this: if it's good enough for an investor then why not for you? Protect yourself and your investment. Know exactly what you are getting into before you sign any cheques or agreements. Like Warren Buffett says, *know your business before you invest.*

Before wrapping up, I have one final story about pricing. I heard a very prominent entrepreneur discussing her experience in setting her prices, *during* her very first sales meeting with her very first customer! She used a technique that she referred to as "flinch pricing". She recounted how she was selling an accounting software package that she produced and when she told the buyer that it would *"cost X dollars"* the buyer didn't flinch, so she quickly added *"per year"*. Again, no flinch so she seamlessly added *"per user"* and the buyer STILL didn't flinch, so she quickly tacked on *"plus support"* but then the buyer did flinch, *a bit*. Next, having picked up on the flinch, she carefully backpedaled, *"BUT, since you're willing to commit today, we can offer free support for the first 3 years"*. Buyer agrees. Mastery! She carefully ratcheted up the price until she detected negative feedback and then subtly back peddled just enough to secure a very attractive price. Was it naiveté or simply beginner's luck? I'm not sure. Could be both; but either way you might want to try this at some point; provided you're very good at reading body language and as cool as Dirty Harry.

Promotion

If the production of your product is the Yin then surely the promoting and selling of it is the Yang. Even though manufacturing and selling are situated on very different locations along the supply chain, they are critically connected. To be successful, you have to master both, and everything in between! So, how do you promote your product or service? Let's explore.

So, what is promotion? The usual response is "inducements" or "giveaways" or "contests" however these are only part of the answer. There are others and collectively they are known as the Promotional Mix which is:

- personal selling

- advertisements

- sales promotions

- public relations

Let's take a closer look at each of these:

Personal Selling

In most businesses, at some point you're going to have to "pound the pavement" because personal selling can play a fundamental part of your success. Personal selling is the vital face-to-face communication between a salesperson and a client about a product or service. In my experience, the degree of success in personal selling is directly co-related to how well one *builds relationships* with clients. Let's suppose that you and a competitor have similar offerings. However your sales techniques are not similar at all. You make it a priority to maintain frequent *direct* lines of communication with potential customers, whereas your competitor occasionally drops off literature and then fades away. When the time comes for the customer to make a purchase, whom do you think gets the call first? Likely you will, because you spent the extra time and effort developing the relationship. Beyond this, I would suggest that when developing relationships with your customers, you pay special attention to the following:

1) You are well advised to not just drop in on you customers without giving them reasonable advance notice *and* receiving their blessing. With your customers dealing with downsizing, juggling multiple objectives and working extended hours a surprise visit by you can totally derail their day. You don't want that responsibility on your shoulders. You would probably be better off catching Yellow Fever than getting the reputation of being the *"drop in guy"* because being so will almost certainly kill your chances of securing their business and even worse; the word about you and your methods will spread. By doing this, you are effectively telling your would-be client: "my time is more important than yours". I went out of my way not to purchase from the "drop in guy". So, be courteous and call *days* in advance to book a brief meeting. Be clear what the meeting objective is and then call the day of the meeting just to make sure that the appointment is still convenient for them.

2) When you actually meet with the client, do not take even one minute longer than you agreed to – and point this out as you are preparing to leave - your customer will appreciate your professionalism, candor and honesty. Convey your message and then say goodbye; it will make a profound impression on him.

3) Make sure that your customers can reach you any time that they need to. You never know when they will need a big favor and big favors often get returned in spades.

4) Be a top of mind resource/problem solver for your customers. Strive to be the first person to whom they turn when they need something done. Eventually your customers will stop looking to your competitors for help and just go the person that can get it done – you.

Before moving onto the next item in the mix, I need to address very quickly personal selling within the context of an online business such as Amazon or a micro version of an Amazon. Clearly, supporting this business model with face-to-face meetings is not practical. To support your online venture, first and foremost you should have a very well designed website that is intuitive, logical and provides immediate answers to any and all foreseeable questions that your customers may have. As a second line of support you might want to consider providing real-time or near real-time feedback to customer concerns. If you make it easy for them to be your customer, they will be loyal. If you don't, you will forever be faced with the formidable challenge of trying to win customers back – a very expensive proposition I assure you. If you lack the resources to respond immediately to your customers, then at the very minimum consider providing a feedback template that they can populate. Next, if you can do it, promise to respond within 24 hours on weekdays. This is a standard that many of the monoliths manage to follow, so it should easily be doable by you. One other thing, actually a pet peeve of mine are feedback templates that have specific categories that you have to check. Nine times out of ten my concern is not listed in the scant choices that are provided. That is really annoying! So, provide your customers with the ability to explain their problem without trying to shoehorn them into some irrelevant category. While I'm on my "template rant", I should add this. If possible, *please* make sure that your web designer doesn't set up your template to dump the populated fields in the event of a field omission or if the customer needs to briefly migrate from the page. Automatically erasing fields is a great way to promote the competition after your customers get frustrated enough to leave the site! Pet peeves done.

Advertisement

Volumes have been written on the subject of advertising, especially with the addition of the Internet and the development of social media, so this primer can at best only scratch the surface of the subject to keep it below 2000 pages.

When deciding on your advertising strategy, there are many issues that must be considered. The top issue regarding advertising for most start-ups, and for going concerns for that matter, is cost versus profit or more formally, ROI (see financial ratios in Accounting). So, let's explore cost-effective approaches to getting the most from your advertising buck. Miserly rule number one: for start-ups, emphasis should be on the Internet as your primary means of advertising as it is arguably the most accessible and cost effective form of advertising for small businesses, especially information-based business models. Later on, if the money starts to roll in, you can consider print media, radio and possibly television. Other possibilities are billboards, movie theatre ads and sporting events. Beyond this, who knows; I wouldn't be surprised to see Apple's logo on the moon one day!

The goal of your advertisements should be twofold:

1) To communicate information on the advantages and the need for your product/service to as many viable customers as possible - called *reach*

2) Making that communication as effective and informative as possible - called *richness*

So, how does one obtain richness and reach on a tight budget? The answer to this question is very much dependent upon the type of business that you run or intend to run. If you run a gardening service or a restaurant, then in *most* cases extended reach is not a possibility because you likely cannot provide services out of your immediate geographical area. The exception to this scenario would be if you scaled your business by franchising your services regionally or even nationally. Then you would have substantially extended your reach. As an aside, scaling the right business in this manner can lead to much improved revenue streams, the proverbial "making money while you sleep" scenario. A nice thought to be sure, but let's crawl before we go supersonic!

It is important at the outset to realize that some business models simply cannot be configured to offer significant reach. This is a very important consideration when thinking about your exit strategy, because without adequate reach, your business will have a very well defined - i.e. <u>limited</u> - upside and therefore will have a limited appeal to potential buyers.

Richness is a measure of the quality of the purchasing experience, the conveyed details about the product and the subsequent understanding that the customer acquires, which is critical to achieving a sale. Depending on your business model, the internet can be a critical tool to help you accomplish the goals of richness *and* reach. Take books being sold on amazon.com as an example. Customers can search out a title/author, see the cover, get information about the number of pages, word count, table of contents, browse some chapters, read customer feedback/reviews, often in the context of a direct comparison with other books, get pricing and shipping information. A very rich experience indeed and Amazon's reach couldn't extend any further. This is a prime example of a company using its website as a key marketing and advertising tool to create its proverbial "front door" to the business. Notice, the key to Amazon's success is a perfect combination of the quality of its content, the vast number of products that it carries and the extensiveness of its reach. So, if you want to leverage the power of the internet using a website as your primary interface to your customers; content quality ***and*** pervasiveness are critical. Let's explore briefly how you can do this.

When I did the first website for my microbrewery (I told you I wore a lot of hats!), I doled out lots of money for Adobe Dreamweaver and lots of money for books on "How to use Dreamweaver" and lots of time learning to program and lots of time programming and lots of time...well, you get the point. Despite the substantial effort and cost, at that time this was a much cheaper alternative to having someone construct the site for me. Also, knowing how the site worked provided me with the ability to make frequent updates at my convenience. Today, the options for web development have grown tremendously for the "layperson" while software costs have plummeted. If I were to create a website today, I would not purchase software because there are a plethora of options available, such as, open source (free!) content management systems (CMS). To construct a CMS driven site, you can choose between Drupal, Joomla and Wordpress just to mention a few. And make no bones about it, by integrating some of the numerous pre-made templates, themes and plug-ins, you can produce a spectacular website simply using drag and drop techniques. Best of all, you don't need to be an expert on MySQL, XHTML, PHP or CSS to do this. Remember, it isn't so much the bell and whistles of your site; it's the quality and thoroughness of your content that counts. Make it comprehensive and dead easy to navigate and your website will generate traffic, provided it has been optimized for browser searches - called *search engine optimization (SEO)*, which we will investigate later. If you prefer not to distract yourself with designing websites and decide to hire a person to build one for you instead, please make sure that they understand SEO. Also, make sure that they set up the site so that *you* are able to do regular updates with ease.

The next thing is your domain name. For example, "janessnazzysneakers.com" or "mikeslawncare.net". Now be warned, finding an address or domain name will likely be a difficult undertaking, especially if you want a *top level domain (TLD)* of ".com". Be patient, be creative and you will eventually find one that is available and appropriate. Finding a name can be done at numerous sites, for example at www.whois.net. You begin the process by going to this site and entering the name that you would like with the TLD of your choice. If you are lucky, your site name and TLD will be available to purchase. If you aren't so lucky, the site will return a list of available and very similar renditions of the names that you have submitted. For example, if you submit *BobsBooze.com* and it is already owned (note, you might be able to buy the rights from the owner if it is not in use) the site may return *BobbysBooze.com* or *BobsBooze.net* or *BobsDrinks.com*, etc. as alternative suggestions. Once you have a found and secured an acceptable URL/TLD, the next step is to find a host. NOTE: some hosts will provide you with a domain free of charge if you use their hosting services. Spend some time researching other people's experiences with the host and decide from there.

The next step in planning your website is to.....plan your website! The old school approach to creating a website was to create several generic informational pages and then link them through a homepage with navigational buttons, go live and then...*hope for the best!* Effectively, websites were an electronic version of a glossy brochure. Well, things have come a long way baby! A much more strategic and holistic approach to website construction and positioning is now the norm; which is the basis of SEO. This means that contemporary websites are far more comprehensive and strategically targeted then they were in the past. For effective advertising using the Internet, you need to embrace this change. When you make your site, you should not limit your target audience to people who already know of your market or even your name, because a significant customer-base for many businesses resides "upstream" from this group at a more general, fundamental level. Let's call them *"upstreamers"*. Upstreamers don't even know that they have a problem to solve and they certainly don't know your company name or its products. This is where *market segmentation* comes in. Market segmentation refers to the "slicing up" of markets into groups that share common attributes. Examples of market segments are: bodybuilders, tweens, males 19 to 25, baby boomers, mullets, foodies, NASCAR fans, entrepreneurs, students, babies and retiree's. You need to create *landing pages* that target various segments of the market, based on their level of engagement and understanding of your market, products and services. Your segments will range from upstreamers to people that know specifically your name/products, plus everyone in between. For the former, this is the furthest point upstream and this is where you efforts should begin. OK, this may sound weird, but your goal for the upstreamer segment is to create landing pages that tell them that *they do indeed have a problem or a need*. If your arguments are sound and your content is well thought out, this can be achieved. There are several approaches to accomplishing this. Some of these approaches may be based on promoting *awareness out of fear*, such as advertisements for hepatitis immunization that target would-be travelers when they are searching for "vacations". Conversely, another approach can be based on benefits instead of fear. For example; pulling traffic to a website for gym equipment that is based on promoting the *personal health benefits* of working out. Pages show up when one is doing a search for "gym equipment". This is the most captive audience and it makes perfect sense that they would land on your site if they are looking for the types of products that you sell. What about the upstreamers that might be searching "health food stores" or "gyms". For a guy selling gym equipment, these are all fair game and easily fall into desirable market segments. For these upstreamers, much more rudimentary pages show up and begin the process of making the connection between health food stores and gym equipment, which really is the art of a well-made website. Next, on the heels of all the benefits that have been pointed out that tie health food stores to gym equipment, the pages *begin* to specify the best types of equipment that will yield various benefits and then finally, direct links to the website/products. You see, it is kind of like a funneling process. At the outset, the net is cast widely and the landing pages are very general and can capture large swaths of many different and desirable market segments. As the focus of the pages gets more specific, there will be many upstreamers that will move on, *but many will not*. Eventually, a small percentage of the upstreamers will convert to purchase the gym equipment. The beauty is that just a short time before these now converted upstreamers didn't even know that they needed gym equipment! But, in reality they actually did need the equipment; and that is what makes it so brilliant. There is no sleight of hand here. It's just skillful marketing that connects two unlikely parties together to engage in commerce.

So, with regard to your site, let's assume that you are going to focus on this *benefits-based approach* when constructing your upstreamers landing pages. When you construct these pages, please bear in mind that you need to present compelling content that draws the attention of the person *immediately* because you probably have about three seconds of scan time before the average person bails on your page if it does not hook. This leads us to keywords and to effective headings. A critical aspect of your website design should be optimizing your site for *search engine crawlers (also called spiders, ants or bots)* such as Googlebot, Yahoo! Slurp or Bingbot. This optimization process is another key aspect of SEO. To summarize, important aspects of SEO include:

1) Optimized keyword choices and headers

2) Brilliant content

3) Numerous links from many other well-ranked websites

4) Age of the site

(Note: I recommend that you look at google.com *Webmaster Tools* for more information on Google's perspective. It is very informative).

It's a challenge, to be sure, but these qualities are critical to having your site rank highly on search engines and draw in the masses. To optimize the keywords you may want to consider using resources such as Google AdWords, Market Samurai or Wordtracker to determine how well your chosen keywords rank. Part of ranking is determined by considering the number of searches conducted for a word or term, over a given time-frame; the number of sites competing for the keywords; the age of these competing sites and the number of links pointing towards a site. Keyword search software is comprehensive and simply too much to address in this primer, so you will need to check out YouTube for tutorials on keyword search software that you have chosen. Invest the time to learn. It will make a big difference in the traffic levels to your site.

Once you have determined the best keywords, make sure that you incorporate them into all of your pages and *in a logical way*, being very careful not intentionally to repeat them, thinking that more is necessarily better: It is not. Keywords must naturally flow through your content, in context and throughout your website. As I mentioned already, your content must be top notch, so deliberately repeating keywords or using them out of context, will not hold you in high favor with ingenious website ranking systems. A fundamental approach to achieving this goal is to create alluring headers as a prelude to very informative and dynamic (updated often) articles about your products or services.

One final aspect to keywords that we need to address is something called *long tail, chunky middle and fat head searches (no! this is not a discussion about my anatomy!).* Before looking at the Search Demand Chart below, please understand the following:

Organizations with very common, generic products (*similar, undifferentiated* in a highly competitive market) are found on the head/middle and will have substantially more hits, but on very few keyword choices (LOTS of competition for few words!! NOT good). Conversely, organizations with very uncommon, unique products (highly differentiated products and very low competition, but small markets) are found on the long tail searches. Conversion rates are much higher for the long tail searches and much lower for the head/middle - a result of high competition at the head/middle and very low completion at the long tail.

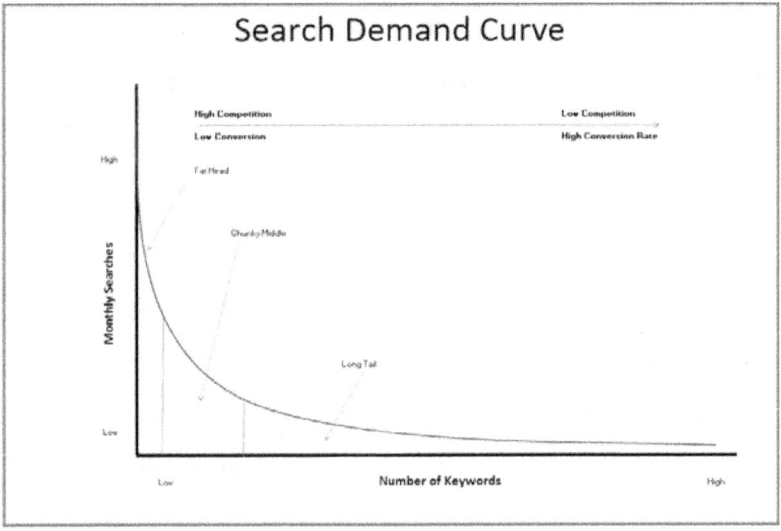

Demand Chart: Search Hits vs. Keywords available

To understand the long tail, you need to make a clear distinction between it and the *fat head* &*chunky middle* by using the above chart to understand the following two scenarios:

1) The fat head/chunky middle searches are associated with businesses that have "few item, big volume" business models, similar to many bricks and mortar (physically tangible) types of businesses. That is, selling many, *many* units of a relatively small number of common products. Think McDonald's - hamburgers, fries and shakes – few products, HUGE volumes! This is largely due to the adoption of simple, easily repeated processes, outstanding quality control and making sure that precious inventory space is limited to relatively few fast-moving items, *not* one sale per year inventory.

2) Conversely, think about a business model where relatively few units of each product are sold, but with many, many *different* products being offered. This is what long tail searches are all about – very product-specific searches. In the end, both business types have revenues that are substantial but sales patterns that are wildly different. Examples of long tail search business models include: Amazon for ebooks, iTunes and Google Music for music and eBay for auction items. Since digital storage is so cheap, reserving "cyber shelf space" for eclectic, one-sale-per-year items does not represent an onerous cost for e-retailers. Can you imagine how large a physical bookstore would need to be to hold *just one* hard copy of every ebook that Amazon carries? Obviously not practical and this is what sales related to the long-tail search are all about. It's the creation of a business model that adds up small amounts of sales on many, many different items. In the end, both scenarios result in the sale of many units, but the difference is that long-tail business models exploit many small, seemingly insignificant markets to their fullest.

So, referring back to Jane's Snazzy Sneakers from the accounting section, let's look at an example. Jane understands the criticality of having *both* the richness and the reach of an amazon.com. Therefore, she augments her bricks-and-mortar business model to allow for an online presence that will extend her business to many more segments. Let's assume that Jane has programmed her website with keywords that *she believes* will create significant traffic. Unfortunately, because of her keyword choices, the bulk of the traffic that will list her on a search will likely be from the head, with its rather generic needs, such as "tennis shoes" or "rain boots". Worse yet, since the head is where the competition lives, if Jane happens to be lucky enough to ever have a searcher click on her site while searching for tennis shoes (*very* unlikely because she will almost certainly *not* rank in the top 25 returns on generic searches, let alone the top three due to intense keyword competition) she will need to deal with that hit very skillfully. Jane's site will need to be set up with <u>many anticipated scenarios</u> to guide traffic through progressively more focused (e.g. tennis shoes > non-marking sole> white>blue stripes) landing pages leading ultimately to a conversion. The key in this case is having many pages programmed that allow Jane to funnel the customer to conversion.

Now let's investigate the opposite scenario. Let's assume that

Jane includes landing pages on her site that cater not only to the head but also the long tail searchers. Imagine a diehard KISS fan who is searching for *"black knee-high studded genuine leather boots with snake fangs"* (I know, I know; WHY?!?!). Google ranks Jane's site as #1 and this person *will* land at Jane's homepage. How did she pull this off? It is due to the specificity and uniqueness of the search and the scant competition for the keywords that gave Jane this auspicious privilege. Jane lists these ridiculously eclectic boots on her site and sells them. Jane, with the possible exception of Gene Simmons, is one of a few people in the world that sells these boots. I bet you are thinking; *"So what did Jane do right to get the sale?"* or *"I thought she was bricks and mortar?"* or *"Isn't following KISS so nineteen seventies?"* Well, Jane was smart because she didn't tie up her precious shelf space with such an eclectic item or thousands of others that she has listed on her site. No: Instead she had made arrangements with a few custom fabricators to have orders processed easily and shipped remotely, but at a premium, of course. She stocks no snake boots (there is something you never hear!) but she does get paid when someone orders them through her site. For each long tail sale, she gets paid handsomely for her efforts because our long-tailed KISS fan, being so overjoyed at finding the boots, is very unlikely to squabble over the price. As far as Jane goes, beyond setting up the website and sourcing a few manufacturers, she actually had to do *nothing* to make the sale or to close it. Being a progressive entrepreneur, Jane didn't rely completely on her bricks-and-mortar business to float the boat. She was shrewd, she was entrepreneurial. Jane saw these limitations of bricks and mortar and decided to scale her business to include an e-business component *as an adjunct* to the retail component. Doing so allowed her to leverage the richness of a well-designed website and the reach of the internet to tap into more distribution channels. Businesses that leverage the benefits of both the bricks and mortar business model and the e-business model increase their chances of success over singular approaches. Strive for this with your business, if possible. The moral of this story? If your business model can utilize the long tail and generate profitable revenues from it, do your best to accommodate this. If you can do all three, the head, the tail and the bricks-and-mortar, as Jane has, then by all means do it. To all KISS fans, I apologize; there is absolutely nothing wrong with snake fanged boots....

The final SEO technique that I want to discuss is establishing links from other sites. Experts in SEO will tell you that these links (quality, *trusted* links) are vital to achieving search engine credibility and high rankings. Speaking of high rankings, did you know that the number one rank on Google's organic searches garners about 40% of the clicks, the number two listing gets about 25% and the third gets about 15% of the clicks? Clearly, you need to strive to be on the first page, preferably within the top three returns. So, how do you get links pointing to your site? Well, you already have a fundamental part of the story sewn up: excellent, relevant and useful content. Without great content, I can assure you that you are dead in the water. By having great content, you set the stage for drawing substantial attention to your site and *keeping* that attention through links to other sites. Consider doing a blog; consider a forum; consider going on other blogs. Work with your suppliers and their sites. If you have other websites, create relevant links to and from each site. Utilize social media; Facebook, Twitter, digg, and Linkedin by creating pages there and, *if allowed*, link to your website and to your blog if you have one. Do your best to be everywhere. Go onto websites for SEO (be careful not to get sucked into those high cost subscriptions!) to find cutting-edge ideas and further optimize your site. Make those search engine crawlers work overtime trying to keep up with your changes. Do this and you will move up the rankings slowly but surely. This is your best bet for 21st century low-budget advertising. As your company grows, you can do the ROI on more conventional advertising avenues.

Sales Promotion

An effective marketing choice - although a potentially expensive one - is point of purchase (POP) items such as posters, brochures and custom displays. Even though POP can be costly, if you approach it with some creativity you can get a really big bang for the buck. When I ran my brewery, I used something called tent cards to promote the business. Tent cards are like mini billboards that one commonly sees on tables at restaurants and bars. The beauty of tent cards is that people just can't help but look at them. Try as you may to not look at them, they tend to draw your eyes in like a moth to light. Using a low-cost color printer, I made my own tent cards, mounted them in plastic holders and then sent them to my draft beer accounts. They actually looked quite professional and the feedback that I received from the accounts was very positive. Based on this success, I decided to step it up and worked with a professional printer to receive a much nicer looking tent card that was printed on superior card stock. In the end, the professionally manufactured tent cards actually came at a *better* price/unit than the hand-made ones – but I did have to commit to a sizable purchase. At this point I didn't mind doling out some cash on such a big and potentially risky purchase because tent cards were now a *proven concept*.

As you can see from this example, the key to sales promotion is to cheaply *test the waters* first whenever possible to get some quality feedback rather than just throwing money at it and hoping for the best. This is *entrepreneurial* thinking. Any time that you can make decisions using *real data*, you are a thousand times better off than rolling the proverbial dice, which as we all know, is gambling, not investing. So, am I telling you that you need tent cards? Well, only in the unlikely scenario that your end-user is a restaurant or bar. No, the point of this story is definitely not to run out and buy tent cards. The point is to make insightful observations on the business environment, appreciate what the current norms are and then explore cost-efficient ways to meet or exceed these norms. Even better, if you can do it, try to find ways to eliminate the norms; completely changing the rules for your industry. Our tent cards did not do this but our nine-pack came pretty close. On my desk I have a copy of a high profile industry publication called *The New Brewer*, that has an article that focused on our nine-pack and pointed out some advantageous aspects of the format over the traditional six-pack or twelve-pack. That didn't hurt our sales!

Other methods of sales promotion, depending on the product/service include:

- POP product samplings (foods, creams, drinks, perfumes..etc.)

- New subscriber inducements: 1 month free, no payments for 1 year, 25% off the first year, etc.

- Coupons (flyers, at POP, mobile, online)

- Mail in rebates

- Contests

- Any creative and cheap way that you can devise to turn people's attention to your product/service

Look at sales promotion as priming the consumer well. As long as you have an innovative product or approach that will get people talking once they try it, then you can view sales promotion as a necessary expense to get the ball rolling. Once that ball does begin to roll and your product starts to take on a life of its own, then you may be able to pull back *somewhat* on sales promotion costs. If, however, you have a commodity-like product that cannot be easily differentiated from your competition's products then you must be prepared to divert a constant flow of money towards sales promotion to keep your product top of mind. Also, with a commodity-like product, there will likely be no buzz about it; no word of mouth promotion about your service. Strive to be different. It will carry you a long way.

Public Relations (PR)

PR is the process of managing the lines of communication between the public and your business. Methods for accomplishing this can be quite similar to advertising (print media, television, radio, Internet). However, contrary to advertising, these efforts carry virtually no cost. If money is tight, you can explore low-cost approaches, which come from guerilla marketing methods. Along with websites, this is my absolute preference during the start-up phase of a business. When my family owned the brewery, one of my partners was listening to the radio and heard a famous radio personality doing "live on the street" conversations with the public. Immediately my partner took a few of cases of our beer to the location of the interviewer and then, with the beer cases in hand, stood conspicuously in the crowd. The host couldn't help but notice her; and the beer. When asked about it, she told him that it was for him. Next, a conversation ensued about the brewery, the family connection, the awards and any other enticing tidbit that she could throw in *live on the air*! Viola! Free radio spot; and a very impressionable one at that because it wasn't scripted or contrived in any way. It was real-time and sincere; quite the opposite of most paid advertisements. This sincerity and honesty is the key to the value of PR. By the way, sales of our product spiked up noticeably after that interview.

Other approaches to PR can be done on forums, podcasts and

blogs. (See prexamples.com for others)

That concludes the four elements of the promotional mix. Now back to the final of the 4P's, which is Place.

Place

Place, the final element of the 4 P's refers to *how* your product gets into your customer's hands (gets to your customer's "place") which is known as the *channels of distribution*. In a way, we have already touched upon distribution channels, particularly for businesses that market primarily over the internet. With regard to distribution channels, information-based companies that distribute over the Internet have a distinct advantage over bricks and mortars by being able to instantaneously distribute their products/service (ebooks, music, software or training materials) worldwide with the click of a mouse. This, from the customer's perspective is perfect for the speed and efficiency of the sale; without their having to get off the couch! From the company's perspective, it is perfect for capturing "need it now" or impulsive purchases. For these business models, the richness of the website's content "makes the sale" and then a payment protocol, such as PayPal closes it.

Before wrapping up Marketing, I would like to make a few

parting comments about bricks and mortar businesses. As I mentioned earlier, bricks and mortars are "physically tangible" businesses, such as grocery stores, home improvement stores and fast food outlets. A critical key to success for strictly B&M businesses is having the potential for a steady flow of walk-in traffic. This implies a requirement to be located within reasonable proximity to a large customer-base. Choosing an isolated location for a B&M business compromises your primary or more likely, your only distribution channel. To optimize your choice for a location, your prospective site should be researched very carefully to ensure that it will give you the best "bang for the buck" that you can possibly afford. Ideally you will have a professional conduct the research for you. However, if you can't afford that, take matters into your own hands and compile some data, *any data* that will help to guide you. Before I selected one of our locations, I chose not to pay for research and instead parked my car beside the property that was under consideration and watched. Eight hours, one medium pizza and two Cokes later, I counted and logged the total number of cars going by. I also logged the type of cars too because I believe that this gave me a quick and dirty demographic study also! Pretty bare bones research, but it was something tangible and much better than just gut feel. Do you remember that treasured real estate tenant about the top three rules on how to select a property? *Location, location, location.* Follow it; it is sage advice.

So, what about manufacturing businesses, distribution companies or storage businesses that don't require an on-premise sales component? Well, businesses that can be located in industrial parks would fall under this category. Industrial-type operations that don't require a retail component typically have much more latitude in a location selection, but they too are not without challenges. The primary challenges for these types of businesses are getting a competitive lease rate *for the duration of the lease* (not just the first year!), getting leasehold improvements done by the landlord, being situated at a close proximity to highways/railways and having good access to labour markets. A real estate agent specializing in industrial buildings can be most helpful if you are in this camp.

I saw recently a beautiful, quaint candy store that had just opened its doors and unfortunately, I knew immediately that the store would be gone within six months. Why? Well, even though the store was located right on a corner of a busy intersection with a stop light, which is usually a good thing, there were some crucial elements missing. First, there was only one parking spot in the immediate area. Second, there were no schools in the immediate area (and not-so immediate area either). Third, there were not a lot of houses nearby. Three strikes and the odds were stacked against the business before it really got going. If the proprietor had asked me for my opinion before securing a location, I would have recommended a much more strategic setting and approach. Once she committed to that location, she effectively gave up her one and only distribution channel and thereby sealed her fate. Sad story; but the location mistake is not uncommon. So, choose your place very carefully and use logic and data, not emotion, providence or hope. As a follow-up, I recently drove by the candy store and the signs are now all gone, the store is dark and empty and a "For Rent" sign is in the window.

PART III
Basics Economics

"Economists are pessimists: they've predicted 8 of the last 3 depressions"

Barry Asmus

So, just how much about economics do you think that one should know to effectively start and run a business? Well, in my humble opinion the answer is, *the more the better.* It is not a prerequisite BUT as an entrepreneur, a basic knowledge of both microeconomics and macroeconomics will serve you very well and could very well give you the upper hand over your competition. Having this knowledge will give you special insight about market spaces, cost of money and pricing issues that your competitors will not likely have. As an overview, we will be addressing the following concepts:

- Supply and Demand

- Price Elasticity of Demand

- Interest rates and central bank's monetary policy

Supply and Demand

I'll bet that you've heard people say something like this before: "Everyone that I know wants to buy and iPad and I do too, but they're just so expensive". This is a great example of supply and demand. The above statement touches on two key aspects of supply and demand: price point and demand. When there is a massive demand for a product; demand so immense that it outstrips the ability of the producer to supply, the result is that the price point typically tends to rise. There is a flip side to that coin though because eventually high prices drive down demand and/or foster competition to achieve what is known as supply/demand equilibrium. This is something that we are starting to see in the market with Android devices taking more of the smartphone and tablet from a market that Apple once dominated. "Supply and demand" simply refers to two concepts that are very much interdependent in any marketplace. Generally speaking, supply refers to the amount of goods that an organization is willing to produce, *contingent on pricing levels*. On the other hand, demand is the amount of a product sought within a market, *contingent on pricing levels*. Clearly, pricing is the linchpin between the two concepts. Is this starting to sound familiar; like déjà vu? As we learned in the Pricing section of Marketing, low prices spur marketplace demand and conversely, low prices are a *disincentive* for manufacturers to produce. A balance or equilibrium needs to be established within an open and competitive marketplace that yields a price that is acceptable to customers *and* provides a reasonable incentive (profit) for the manufacturer. Remember that Price-Volume Relationship graph from the Pricing section? What you saw there was actually a Supply-Demand graph with a few minor adjustments. Look at the following graph (same graph as before, but with the axes relabeled):

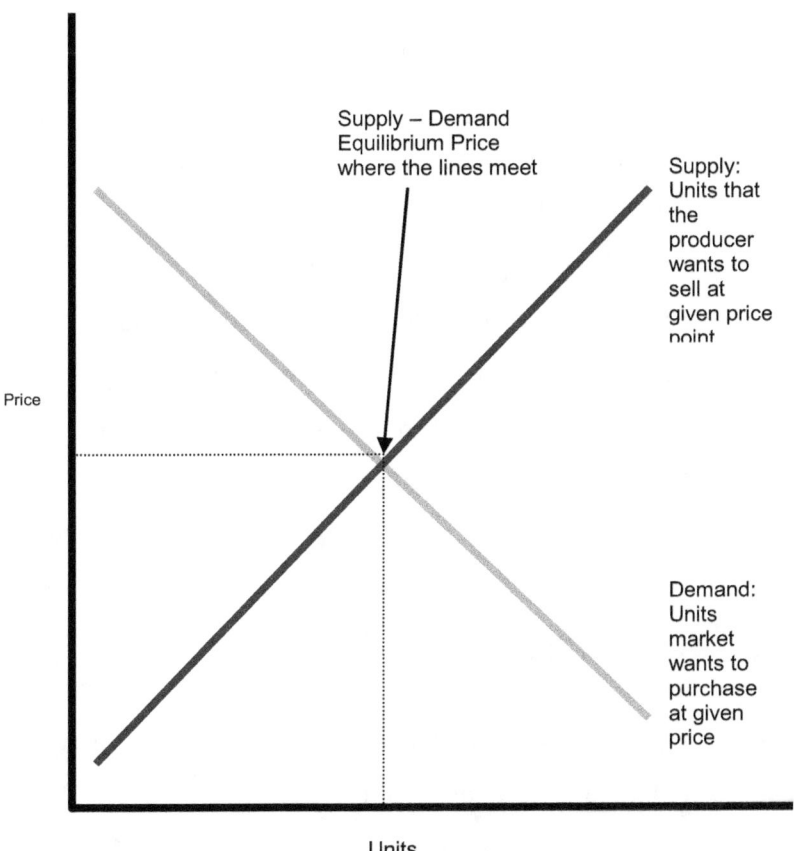

Supply – Demand Equilibrium Price where the lines meet

Supply: Units that the producer wants to sell at given price point

Price

Demand: Units market wants to purchase at given price

Units

The Supply Demand Model

Supply-Demand curves

For your purposes, finding your product's price point equilibrium should be your key objective. Note, despite the eloquence of the above model, it is neither reasonable nor practical to try to find a discrete price point as indicated at the intersection of the two graphs. A small range of prices is likely as precise as you are going to get. As you go through price changes, you will get a better feel of what the supply/demand "curve" (there is actually a slight bend to each graph) looks like for your specific business, which will help you establish your price point equilibrium. Speaking of price changes, this provides us with a nice segue into the next topic, which is Elasticity of Price Demand.

Price Elasticity of Demand

This topic can become very daunting very quickly since a *technically* complete understanding of the topic requires the use of messy things like differential equations. Well, here's the good news. I am going to show you exactly what you need to know, without any calculus getting in the way. *Price elasticity of demand* refers to the effects that price changes have on the demand of a product or service. According to our economist friends, there are five basic market responses to a price *increase*:

1) No change in demand from price increase; called "perfectly inelastic demand" and revenues will rise dramatically

2) Small drop in demand compared to price increase: "relatively inelastic demand" and revenues will rise somewhat

3) Demand drops proportionally to price increase: "unit elastic demand" and revenues remain unchanged

4) Demand drop is greater than price increase: "relatively elastic demand" and revenues drop

5) Demand drops significantly from any price increase: "perfectly elastic demand" and revenues plummet!!

So, immediately after a price increase for your product, you need to carefully monitor if the demand changes. Now here is the doomsday scenario for a price increase: If a 1% price hike results in a 10% *reduction* in sales, called relatively elastic demand, then you must revisit your decision quickly. For whatever reason (undifferentiated product? many competitors?) your market is extremely price sensitive and that is going to present some challenges. Relatively elastic demand is not a welcome response to a price increase and if this is the result of your price increase, you might want to focus much more intensely on cost reductions and product differentiation as opposed to price increases. Another angle to consider in cases that have such exaggerated price dependencies is to do some math on price *decreases*. Sounds counterintuitive right? Well if a 1% price increase elicits a 10% drop in sales, then perhaps a 1% drop in price could *increase* sales by 10%. You never know. Fully investigate all of the scenarios.

The most likely result of a price increase is a *proportional* drop in demand. This is what is predicted by the previously shown supply-demand graph and is known as *unit elasticity*. Intuitively, this makes sense because when prices increase, a certain segment of the market can no longer justify the purchase. Per the law of supply and demand, at higher prices, the producer is willing to produce more (more profit!); but is *typically* not able to sell as many units due to reduced demand. These are handy facts for those times that you cannot meet demand and cannot afford to expand. All that you need do is simply bump up your prices (just a bit, you don't want to encourage competition!) and demand *should* fall to more manageable levels.

What you should be hoping for, and what I have seen during early cycles (i.e. very new company) of price increases is a much smaller drop in demand *proportional* to my price increase. This result was the best of both worlds for me because it ended up rewarding me with the dual benefit of increased revenues and somewhat attenuated volumes; which in turn made keeping up with my production obligations less difficult. Put another way, I got to work less to make more money.

I have also experienced *no drop* in demand after a price increase (*perfectly inelastic*) – which is really a dream come true for any small business. To explain this phenomenon I reasoned that since I held such a minute percentage of the total market share, conventional economic models simply didn't apply. Either way, I was very happy indeed.

Although not shown in the summary list above, there is another possible result of a price increase that completely contravenes the supply-demand model. This is a scenario where a price increase would result in an *increase* in demand (within limits of course); which does happen in some very rare cases. This is known as a Veblen Good. (*Note there is some confusion between Veblen Goods and Giffen Goods. Giffen Goods are inferior goods [less demand as consumer income rises], have no direct substitutes and do not follow the standard supply-demand curve*). An example of a product that I would consider a Veblen Good is the beer Stella Artois. The beer seemed to take on this status as a result of a very slick advertising campaign that deemed the product "reassuringly expensive". The advertisement positioned the beer as a *status symbol*, as opposed to a product belonging to a market segment that is widely - and mistakenly - viewed as a commodity. Stella's positioning was ingenious because it changed a normally simple cost-to-value decision into an emotional decision. People are willing to pay extra money for status symbols. Whether people will admit it or not, owing and displaying status symbols strokes the ego. Products, like Rolex watches, BMW's or Cristal Champagne come to mind, all of which are very expensive but *not necessarily* equal to their perceived value. That is, they aren't necessarily a superior product to other similarly priced or even lower priced products on the market. Note to German car aficionados. Don't shoot the messenger! I am just summarizing what many car experts have said. If your product shows evidence of being a Veblen Good after you have gone through several price changes then all that I can say to you is CONGRATULATIONS! You are creating a valuable brand indeed!

Interest rates, Central Banks and Macroeconomics

Of all of the topics in the book, this is probably the most theoretical, but I encourage you to work through it as it will give you a better picture of how macroeconomics can have a significant influence on your business. Also, you will sound really cool at parties when you discuss things like *"that expansionary monetary policy by the Fed is diluting the yields on my bond portfolio."* *Well……..*on second thought, maybe you don't want to do this at parties, unless you're at Thurston Howell the VIII's house.

Have you ever wondered why interest rates seem to meander up and down with very little rhyme or reason? If so, then you may find this section of……..*interest.*

The monetary policies of the world's central banks (e.g. U.S. Federal Reserve, The People's Bank of China, The Bank of England, Deutshe Bundesbank, The Bank of Canada, The Bank of Japan to name a few) act as fundamental drivers for how much it costs to borrow money, or more specifically, *how much it will cost you to borrow money for your business.* Central banks, work in lock-step with federal governments to control the money supply of nations and they do this through adjusting the prime lending rates to commercial banks, buying/selling government bonds and announcing expansionary or contractionary monetary policy. In times when the economy is red hot, prices for products and services tend to rise. This is known as inflation. Central banks have very specific targets for inflation rates and their ability to control rates is through something known as the monetary transmission mechanism (MTM). The monetary transmission mechanism explains the steps that take place with central banks to expand or contract the economy and how that trickles down to your company. Let's look at an example of an expansionary monetary policy using the MTM and something called fractional reserve banking.

Suppose that the economy has been in the dumps and the government and the central bank intend to stimulate the economy because doing so will reduce unemployment, increase tax revenues and increase the nations GDP. Stimulation begins when the central bank signals an expansionary monetary policy through government bond price increases. These increases have the effect of reducing the bond yields thus making the selling of bonds to the bank more attractive than holding them. The selling of bonds by the populace stimulates the flow of money from the central bank to the people as government bonds are purchased. That is the first part of the MTM: Moving money to the populace by affecting changes to bond prices. The next trick up the proverbial sleeve of the central bank is to increase the money supply by lowering prime lending rates. The bank will reduce the prime lending rate to commercial banks, and these banks *should* pass the lowered interest rates onto customers in the form of business loans. With access to lower cost money, the money supply flows to the populace and the process of business stimulation takes hold as start-ups and established businesses borrow money for infrastructure improvements and capital projects. As an aside, QE or *quantitative easing* refers to other mechanisms for economic stimulation, such as printing more money. QE specifically refers to stimulus that takes place in in an already low interest economy. Opponents of QE cite the risk of increased inflation and the adoption of high risk securities by the central banks as red flags to the process.

Fractional Reserve Banking

So what happens when you actually do get a business loan from a bank? Let's look at an example.

Suppose Jane of Jane's Snazzy Sneakers borrows $40,000 and matches it with her own $10,000 for the purchase of a new machine, which she believes is going to help her make a lot of money. The company that built the machine receives $50,000 from Jane and then deposits that money into their bank account. The bank that holds the $50,000 isn't obliged to keep that money tied up in an account. On the contrary, the bank is only obliged, under something called the *fractional reserve banking system*, to hold a minimum reserve ratio; the minimum cash on hand proportional to the size of the deposit. Some countries have reserve ratios as low as zero! The philosophy behind zero reserve is that *deposit insurance* will suffice as a reasonable back up against the worry about lost deposits and it also allows more money to be pushed out to the populace rather than sitting in a vault. In the United States the Federal Reserve mandated reserve ratio is about 10%. So, assuming a reserve ratio is 10%, the bank is free to lend out $45,000 of the $50,000 that was deposited by Jane's equipment manufacturer and must hold back $5,000 in reserves. If another business borrows this $45,000 from the bank and adds $15,000 cash for the purchase of a $60,000 machine then the company that they purchased from then deposits the money into another bank, then under the same reserve ratio, this bank must hold back $6,000 and can lend out $54,000. So I think that you can see what is happening with this; the amount that can be borrowed gets bigger and bigger. First it was $40K, then $45K and then $54K. This process of value creation is known as *deposit multiplication*. It may seem strange to have generated so much commerce from what was originally a $40,000 loan. However this system is based on the principle that banks almost never need to ante up all of their cash deposits at any one time. If, for some very unusual reason, there were a mass withdrawal of cash at a bank, the central bank or other banks could provide fast reserve-covering loans.

Okay, so what in the world does this madness have to do with your small business? Well, it's about timing and in particular, *timing for loans.* Over time the economy tends vacillate up and down, despite the efforts of the central banks. If you set up shop on the heels of a hot economy, you have to plan, and be ready for, an eventual economic slowdown. I'm not being pessimistic; it is just the business cycle. During times of economic slowness there can be a protracted time when accessing loans is difficult, expensive or both. Just be aware of the business cycle when you are getting ready to start and plan accordingly for future financing. In short, borrow the money when you can because in an economic slowdown, you will be subjected to very high interest rates; that's if you can even qualify for a loan in the first place. Macroeconomics done.

Basic understanding of the supply chain

The supply chain is a straight forward enough concept and one that should be reviewed as it will help you to achieve a unique perspective on your business. The supply chain includes all of the parties that play a role in meeting your customer's needs. For manufacturing companies, business-to-business (B2B) distributors and business-to-customer (B2C) retailers, the supply chain typically includes suppliers, inbound logistics, in-house processes, outbound logistics and marketing, which in the end leads to profit. To maximize your overall profitability, you need to ensure that you maximize the profitability of each of these steps. It's been said that you can't manage what you haven't measured, and I strongly agree. You would be wise to define, measure and monitor your key performance indicators (KPIs) along each stage of the supply chain and review them often so that you improve the effectiveness and efficiency of each one. Some companies choose to integrate vertically, which means expanding their ownership of the various steps along the supply chain. For example, instead of using a transport company, they vertically integrate by purchasing their own fleet of vehicles to take care of inbound and outbound logistics. Companies like Anheuser Busch go much further by becoming their own raw material supplier. Can you imagine a brewery making its own cans? Well, by so doing they pocket the profit that the can producer would have made. Let's not get too far ahead of ourselves though; this is major leagues stuff. Vertical integration is generally not for start-ups. For your business, be sure you eke out every penny of waste possible when establishing your supply chain. I will give you a few tips on this process when we look at the fundamentals such as Lean operations and Six Sigma.

Basic understanding of the value chain

As you may have inferred from the name, the *value chain* refers to the process steps that create value for your customer. Manufacturers take raw materials and input labour to perform value-added processes on these raw materials and this is what the value chain is all about. For businesses seeking to maximize profitability, the value chain should be a primary focus area. Manufacturing improvement methodologies, such as Lean Six Sigma, provide proven approaches for reducing process waste and variation along the value chain. These process improvement methods are used by manufacturers in most segments and by health care providers; banks and governments. In short, any organization that utilizes processes can benefit greatly from using Lean Six Sigma. Delving into the minutia of Lean Six Sigma would make this a much longer book, so I won't do that. I will, however, whet your appetite for learning more about it by outlining the fundamental philosophy that it is built upon, *the DMAIC process*. DMAIC is an acronym for the words, Define, Measure, Analyze, Improve and Control, which are the five steps to implementing the system. Each of these steps defines one of the unique stages undertaken to make processes run more efficiently. The following is a very brief overview of each of the DMAIC steps (note: if you believe that you will have no need for Six Sigma, please feel free to push onto the next section):

The D-M-A-I-C Process

DEFINE delineate and characterize the process and the problem that you want to improve. The tools and techniques used in this step are process maps, value stream maps, fishbone diagrams, cause-and-effect matrices, Pareto charts, critical to quality trees, SIPOC diagrams, quality function deployment and affinity diagrams.

MEASURE the process with the most accurate and accessible metrics possible. Examples include times studies; weights, defects per million opportunities, color, customer complaints per million, gauge R&R studies, quantity right first time and defects per million opportunities

ANALYZE the data that you measured (statistical methods, Pareto Charts, histograms, control charts, hypothesis testing, designed experiments, failure mode and effects analysis, 5 Why's, spaghetti diagrams)

IMPROVE the process in the areas that the data analysis indicates deficiencies using designed experiments, real-time process monitoring, data acquisition technology, added supervision, new equipment, different raw materials

CONTROL the process variables to keep the process within acceptable ranges using statistical process control, standardized processes, hypothesis testing and control plans.

There is a plethora of other tools and techniques that you can look up and learn about if you choose to undertake the DMAIC process (or any part of the process) if you so desire. As I'm sure you'll agree, Lean Six Sigma is pretty advanced stuff. Nevertheless you may want to pursue it further as well as other methods for improving supply chain efficiencies such as total productive maintenance (TPM), total quality management (TQM) or Reliability Centered Maintenance (RCM).

PART IV
Business Strategy

"The essence of strategy is choosing what not to do."
— *Michael E. Porter*

Strategy is full of terms and expressions that will likely seem foreign to you at the outset. Therefore, I encourage your patience as you read this chapter. Eventually, these terms and expressions will become absorbed into your vocabulary and you'll wonder how you ever got by without them.

The term *strategy* is ubiquitous in business; perhaps overused and clearly misunderstood by many. Notwithstanding the fact that certain terms originating from business strategy fall into the popular vernacular and become the business "word of the month", strategy is much more than fancy terms and catchy phrases. There is considerable value in learning about it, so let's start by defining it. Johnson and Scholes, in their classic text, *Exploring Corporate Strategy*, define strategy as *"the direction and scope of an organization over the long term, which achieves advantage for the organization through its configuration of resources within a changing environment and to fulfill stakeholder expectations"*

So, who are these stakeholders that J&S refer to? Well, generally speaking, they are your customers; your suppliers; your employees; your investors/partners, your community and of course, you. They are all of the people who have a vested interest in the business that you are starting. J&S also refer to another key issue in their definition, which is *advantage*. I mentioned *advantage* or more specifically, *competitive advantage* in the Product section of Marketing. Competitive advantage actually refers to two other types of advantage: comparative advantage and differential advantage. Comparative advantage refers to the efficiency of your operations versus those of your competitors. Differential advantages are the unique things that separate you from your competitors and allow your business to outperform the competition as a result. Your competitive advantage is your hedge, your leg up on your competitors. So, how do you get this leg up? Let's look at the tools that are used to help evaluate the competition and from that, begin to establish your competitive advantage. Note: I may use the term *strategic advantage* or *strategic competitive advantage* in place of competitive advantage. For our needs, all these terms are synonymous.

SWOT analysis

SWOT analysis is a tool that is used to identify both the internal and the external business environment. The internal aspect refers to you, your ideas, your processes and your team. The external aspect refers to the market space that you intend to enter and the specific competition that you will be facing. The acronym SWOT stands for:

S – Strengths related to you, your team and your organization (internal)

W – Weaknesses related to you, your team and your organization (internal)

O – Opportunities within the business environment that can lead to greater growth and profitability potential (external)

T – Threats that exist in the business environment that could potentially harm the business (external)

The application of a SWOT analysis to your business or business idea and to yourself is your first step in applying strategy. Let's try an example of a SWOT analysis using the previously discussed lawn care business. To remind you of the scenario, let's suppose that you own a lawn care business in a relatively crowded market, and that you have acquired an extraordinary amount of knowledge on the subject of lawn care and soil chemistry. Using this knowledge, you developed and patented a proprietary organic weed treatment offered by no one else. The following matrix shows the result of a SWOT analysis on your product/service and on the competitive environment in which your business operates.

	Helps Organization	Hinders Organization
Internal	**Strengths** ▲ Proprietary knowledge ▲ Deep knowledge of landscaping ▲ Good understanding of competition ▲ First mover advantage ▲ Patent protection ▲ Better people skills than your competitors	**Weaknesses** ▲ Sole proprietorship (limited resources, personal liability) ▲ Financial wherewithal to scale business ▲ Start-up means little revenue at beginning (i.e. Valley of Death) ▲ Will the chosen price point be acceptable to the marketplace ▲ Limited ability to defend patent against a deep pocketed infringer
External	**Opportunities** ▲ People with weeds on lawn ▲ People with perfect lawns (that want to keep them that way) ▲ Golf courses ▲ Parks ▲ Schools and daycare ▲ Graveyards ▲ Sports fields ▲ Franchising ▲ Licensing formula ▲ Selling formula for lump sum or royalties ▲ Large fertilizer company that may want to form strategic partnership	**Threats** ▲ Reverse engineering the lawn treatment formula and creating a knock-off ▲ New more knowledgeable competitors ▲ Large fertilizer companies that can afford to challenge a patent ▲ Long-term efficacy of product ▲ New landscaping trends that don't involve grass

SWOT analysis: Lawn care business

This SWOT took me about 7 minutes to complete so you can imagine how much detail that you could provide on a SWOT of your own business with more time and perhaps a team to commit to the exercise. This is a fantastic tool for building internal and external strategies and creating ready-made plans to deal with various scenarios before they happen. That is strategy! Create a SWOT analysis before you start up and each year after that to keep it aligned with internal and external business environments as they evolve. A SWOT will help to keep your business centered and give you a road map to follow if things….no, *when* things get tough. A logical segue at this point would be to introduce the PEST analysis; however this will be addressed in the Decision Making primer. Feel free to jump to that section read it and then return back here for the grand finale: the gold standard for creating strategy and understanding the competitive environment: *Porter's Five Forces Model.*

Porter's Five Forces Model

When Michael Porter of the Harvard Business School developed the five forces model (FFM) in the late 1970's, it helped to revolutionize the process of strategy development. Possessing a good understanding of this model and how to use it can give you a definite leg up on the competition, so you should invest the time to learn it. To begin the process of learning the model, consider the following simplified diagram of the FFM.

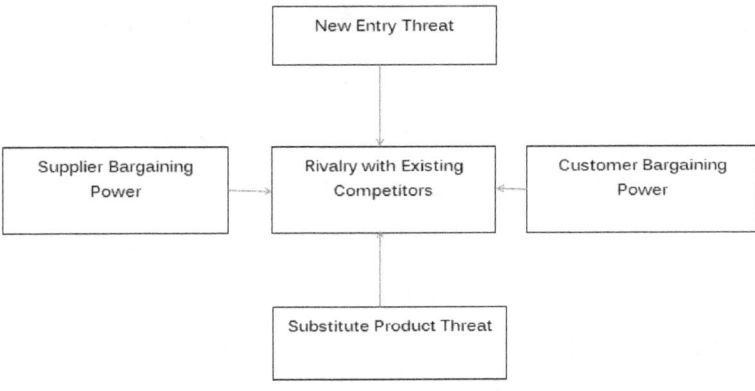

Porter's Five Forces Model

When you look at the Porter's Model, pay particular attention to the Supplier Power and the Customer Power boxes, because I believe that for a start-up, this is where the action is. While the remaining three boxes, Substitutes, Rivalry and New Entrants are important, in my opinion, they present less of a concern during the start-up phase and become much more important once you are established.

So, let's begin with Supplier Power. Because you are a start-up, a complete unknown with no history or long-term rapport with your suppliers, they will likely wield significant power over you, and double that if only a few suppliers ("concentrated") exist. Your job – and this is the key - is to try to reduce Supplier Power by negotiating with them to establish favorable pricing and payment terms. This is not to say that this will be easy for a start-up. Actually, it may not be possible at all. However, for the sake of your cash flow, you need to try. Think of this: you truly have nothing to lose if you aren't successful and much to gain if you are. At the other extreme of Porter's Supplier Power is the scenario where there is widespread competition amongst many suppliers. You should be able to use this situation easily to your advantage by playing the suppliers off of each other to help push pricing and terms to your benefit. Having the ability to substitute your supplier's products with something else shifts power away from your suppliers. For example, a soft drink producer having the option of using cans instead of bottles, shifts power away from bottle suppliers.

Customer Power, the power wielded by your customers over you may present some major challenges. As a start-up, when your product first appears in the marketplace, you start off with ZERO customers, ZERO revenues....yikes! At this point, when you are doing your best to entice customers to switch from established brands to yours, the customer wields ALL of the power. This is the stage that you must woo your customers. It is critical, at this point, to make your product irresistible to the customer. Be creative, be patient, be different and be everywhere that you can possibly be. Be aware though, that as the "new kid on the block", you will be under the microscope and will need to plan strategies to contend with this or even turn it to your advantage. You will need to know your competition intimately, know their products, their prices, their customers, their resources and most importantly, know *them*. If your intention is to get into business without fully understanding your competition, you could very easily lose your investment. Be careful.

Customer Bargaining Power is established in several ways; one of the most important is tied to the number of competitors that exist in the market relative to the number of potential customers. If the potential customer-base is effectively unlimited compared to the number of producers (you and your competitors), then customer power is low. If, however, the scenario was reversed and there were very few customers, and many competitors, then I suggest you cut and run! If you don't, you will be going headlong into a competitive nightmare against many established firms; very possibly competing for table scraps.

Another thing that you must consider is the nature of the products that you offer. If your products are sustainably differentiated from your competitor's, then customer power is reduced because they will have no one else to turn to if they want a product like yours. It pays to be different.

Another consideration in strategy theory is something called *Barriers to Entry (B2E)*. B2E address how easy or hard it is for new competition to get into a particular business. B2E are those pre-existing conditions or the provisions that have been taken to discourage others (and you!) from entering an industry and competing. High B2E reduces the threat of new entrants while low or no barriers invite stiff competition. A prime example of a high B2E is *switching costs*. Switching costs are the costs that customers incur if they decide to stop doing business with a company. Examples would be proprietary software or hardware that is incompatible with your competitions; which helps to "lock in" customers. Cellular phone companies use switching costs to their advantage by locking phone hardware to their systems exclusively and require a fee for unlocking to move to the competition. A large fee will de-motivate a lot of people from going to the competition.

Other notable B2E's would be very high capital costs for start-up, patented processes/products or very specialized knowledge or skills that few have; also known as knowledge asymmetry. To reduce the likelihood of new entrants raining on your parade, take *reasonable* measures to put up as many barriers to entry as possible; but don't preoccupy yourself with it. Focus on revenues first.

In summary, Porter's five forces model provides a methodical approach for analyzing a potential business or industry. Take the time to use it. It could help to prevent you from making a bad investment, and it could help to unveil a golden opportunity.

PART V
Decision Making Skills

"Decision is a sharp knife that cuts clean and straight; indecision, a dull one that hacks and tears and leaves ragged edges behind it."- Gordon Graham

Your decision making ability will, over time, either make or break your business. Sounds harsh, but it is simply a fact. If you don't believe me consider the effects of some bad decisions:

- Bank of America's five dollar debit card charge resulted in a 150,000 strong petition plus 650,000 people switching bank activity to credit unions on a day of protest. Ouch! Bad decision...

- In 1985, the Coca-Cola Company took their proven and coveted formula and tossed it aside for a new formula, dubbed the New Coke. Due to massive public outrage, approximately three months later, the original product was brought back. Double Ouch!! Really bad decision…….

- Ford Edsel. Need I say more?

- Enron's unethical accounting practices foolishly undertaken to hide losses; triple ouch and game over for them.

While these examples pertain to big business, it is important to realize that small businesses have much less staying power than monoliths when it comes to making bad decisions. Big businesses, on the other hand, *generally* have the economic critical mass to weather many more bad decisions. Therefore, the average start-up will be entitled to only so many missteps before the business succumbs. There are many more examples of start-ups making terminal strategic missteps versus start-ups that prosper quickly and painlessly as the result of good decision making. So, as a small business owner, when you make decisions, it is in your best interest to hit home runs as often as possible to avoid being a bad decision statistic. Now, let's look at the tools and techniques that you can use to help make sound, justified decisions.

Weighted spreadsheet

A weighted spreadsheet is a remarkably useful tool for paring down a lot of seemingly good options and choosing the best one. Let's look at an example of the various proposed projects at Jane's Snazzy Sneakers. Jane has a budget to support only one of four proposed projects, so she needs a mechanism to choose the best of the four. She lists all of the potential projects on rows in the first column and then lists decision criteria categories along the top row of each remaining column. This might sound confusing so please look briefly at the spreadsheet below before reading on. Note that each *decision criterion* is given a numerical weighting based on its strategic importance to the company, which was determined by using SWOT, PEST, Porter's Five Forces and cash-flow scenario analyses such as NPV, tweaking cost and revenue estimates and looking for scenarios with the most "low hanging fruit". Using these analyses Jane weighted the different categories, such as: "Floor Traffic Generation" at 40% and the category "Up Front Costs" at 15%.

For each project, ratings that are given are then multiplied by their respective category weightings and then added up. This

summation is the score for each category and the *project having
the <u>highest</u> (i.e. high = greatest benefit to the business) score
wins.* OK, I realize that this sounds terribly confusing, so please
look at the spreadsheet again to see how all this works:

Category	Up front costs (highest = 1, lowest = 10)	Variance in calculated ROI scenarios (1= highest variance, 10=lowest variance)	Customer convenience	Employee Headcount reduction (1=lowest reduction, 10=highest reduction)	Floor traffic generation	Totals
Weighting (%)	15	10	10	25	40	100
Project						
4 Self-scanning check-out areas	2	5	9	9	2	4.75
10 area specific flat screen TV's plus content describing products	3	6	8	7	3	4.8
3 Larger lighted billboards	6	9	3	1	10	6.35
New customer acess shelving	7	4	8	8	4	5.85

SPREADSHEET ANALYSIS: Jane's 4 Project Choice

The methodology for actually populating the spreadsheet was
to look at the project title, look at the corresponding category
and then assign a number from one to ten into the box. So, for
the project "3 larger lighted billboards" and category "Floor
Traffic Generation" a rating of ten was assigned by Jane. The
same approach was used to populate the entire spreadsheet.
Next the column on the far right, titled "totals" was calculated.

Let's take a closer look at how these final numbers were calculated by focusing on just one of the projects. Specifically, the calculation for the "4 Self-scanner checkout" project is as follows:

$$2 \times 15/100 + 5 \times 10/100 + 9 \times 10/100 + 9 \times 25/100 + 2 \times 40/100 = 4.75$$

Very simple, but the results are powerful indeed! As you can see, Jane has taken four projects in five categories, which equates to 20 different possibilities (4 x 5 = 20) and calculated a single highest number: 6.35. *Conclusion: Jane should proceed with the "3 Lighted Billboards" project.*

Lotus blossom

If the weighted spreadsheet is my favorite for pairing ideas down, then the Lotus Blossom Diagram (LBD) is my favorite for idea generation. Creating a LBD is a fascinating procedure because it forces you to think in very different ways than you likely have been taught. After years of troubleshooting/problem solving, which is what most people do, all day, every day, people become almost exclusively accustomed to relying on rote, visceral responses to solve problems. Visceral or kneejerk responses to problems are a double edged sword. On the positive side, they allow for rapid problem solving, but on the negative side, they circumvent the creativity process and increase the risk of implementing non-optimized solutions. Decision making by rote fosters a "one size fits all" approach to problem solving and here is the crux of the problem: previous solutions to problems can't always be effectively "shoehorned" around new problems. So, for critical "make or break it", "show stopping" problems – you should consider using the lotus blossom diagram.

Let us suppose that a young man wants to start up a restaurant, however, he has no idea about how to brand the company and the products; he is just determined to start the business. Understandably, many people in this situation would look immediately at what the competition is doing; especially if some of these competitors are cleaning up with a unique product or approach. Caught up in the spirit of competition - this is the visceral, "knee jerk" part - this person is likely going to think, "I can do *that* even better than they can!" Under the naive belief that he will eat his competitor's lunch, he starts up and produces his rendition of the competition's unique products; BAD MOVE! This is that emotion thing that I touched upon before! Yes, if one tries to copy the competition, this will start the revenue flow....but how much and for how long? Will the grazers try it out once and then move along? Will the market disparage him for copying a competitor? What if the products and brand are deemed no better or heaven forbid, *worse* than the competitors? It is a very risky decision to be sure. Now, imagine yourself in the same situation; what would you do? Rather than adopting this type of non-innovative, deliberately competitive strategy, perhaps you would consider trying a different approach.........(drumroll please) *the lotus blossom diagram*. The LBD that I have shown below considers a brewery start-up. Have a quick glance at the completed LBD before continuing on.

The technique begins with writing down "Issues for brewery start-up" (or the name of your start-up) in the centre box of a grid of boxes. Next, in the boxes surrounding the centre box, write down any of the characteristics that are critical to starting the business that you are planning. Next you take each of the surrounding boxes and do another lotus diagram for each one of these, working your way from the centre box outward (i.e. see financing in the top left). See below for the actual diagram.

sources	amount required	cost of service	rural and ship	unit or indep. Building	tourist area	Brewpub	brewery with tied house	just brewery
equity/debt	Financing	NPV, IRR	local and retail	Location		malt extract	business model	soda
margins	financial ratios	Pro-forma sales	high end boutique	low end factory		sell spent grain and yeast	co-packing	high end, high margin or cost leader ship
monthly excise	payroll	phones	Financing	Location	business model	Porters 5 forces	SWOT	PEST
daily orders	administrative	logistics	administrative	Issues for brewery start-up	team/competitors	Team experience	team/competitors	NO EGOS!!
equipment's purchases	licenses		plant design	market focus	product(s)	ability to work and TRUST each other	brewer, business specialist, experienced sales	
Scalable plant design	Excess capacity for future	Old school/modern	market holes	competitive advantage	younger demographic (college crowd)	Geographical connection	personality connection	cans, bottles or kegs or all three
lowest cost producer	plant design	no plant, contract brew instead	mature/professional demographic	market focus		Lagers or ales or both	product(s)	
pasteurizer			sporting events	bars/home consumption		Which style (pilsner, IPA, ?)	light or dark beers	carbonated or nitrogenized

Lotus Blossom Diagram for a Brewery Start-up

This example shows effectively dozens of potential business plans on one page! Once the diagram is done, then you can maximize your businesses potential by methodically moving from block to block and optimizing each of your selections. How far you go is up to you. There is no set limit on where you need to stop. You can keep moving outward until you have tapped yourself out of ideas. It is eloquently simple, yet very powerful. Now, depending on what your specific goal is, the results of the Lotus Blossom will vary significantly. The results will range from just organizing your thoughts, to the creation of an innovative breakthrough. Just let your creativity flow – that's the key. If applicable, have your partners populate their own diagram independently and then compare. It is a wonderful tool for creatively exploring ideas.

SWOT

When we discussed SWOT earlier, we used it to solve the problem of strategy. We won't delve into another specific example but be aware that in addition to creating strategy, SWOT can be applied to virtually any critical decision.

PEST

PEST is an acronym for Political, Economic, Social and Technological. So, when applying a PEST analysis, you view your problem through each of these lenses. Let's think back to the lawn care business example and the decision of whether to pursue the selling of organic weed treatment services.

Political: Ask yourself the following: Is there government (federal, state/provincial, municipal) legislation or agencies that place restrictions on organic based weed treatments? Are there rigorous definitions of what is deemed organic? Do the people in your market frown upon the use of chemical based weed treatments? Does the media in your area support and promote the use of sustainable green technologies? These are some of the relevant political issues that could affect your business. There are positive effects too. For example, issues like supporting local charities or sports teams, which could be seen positively both politically and socially.

Economic: Is cost of borrowing going down (i.e. expansionary monetary policy)? Are the costs of goods going up (inflation, supply and demand)? Is your chosen market in the embryonic stages, in the growth stage, mature or in decline? Is consumption going up or down? Have substitute products usurped your market?

Social: Are your lawn care products 100% safe for the general public? If you believe they are safe, can you prove it? Are natural gardens, natural lawns and sophisticated landscaping starting to displace manicured lawns? Are people starting to take care of their lawns themselves as opposed to contracting out?

Technological: Has Scott's already invented a green-based substitute for your product? Have new grass strains been developed that can successfully outcompete weeds? What are the long-term effects of the product? Does its efficacy fade over time?

There will likely be a bit of overlap between the findings of the SWOT and the PEST, however there is also a good chance that you will discover something completely unique. The greatest value of the PEST analysis is that it provides a simple and methodical approach to exploring ideas and it does it from a predominately external perspective. One could even say that it is like having the devil's advocate without having to put up with the devil's advocate - they're always so smug and negative aren't they?

Brainstorming

Brainstorming is a technique with which many people are familiar with. Brainstorming involves a group effort to creatively tackle a problem. Despite its usefulness, there are inherent problems with the traditional approach to brainstorming, particularly for introverted people. For people that have a quiet nature about them, speaking up may be difficult. The fallout from this problem is that the brainstorming session may be hijacked by the most vocal members of the group and lead to *groupthink*. Groupthink is a phenomenon in which people either consciously or subconsciously agree with the majority of the group – the path of least resistance. Allowing groupthink gives license to the most vocal members to guide the team's choices to their favor and stymies true collaborative creativity. To be as successful as possible, make sure that brainstorming sessions are facilitated by a person who understands group management. I recommend that each person is not only given a chance to contribute, but is *obliged* to contribute, speaking freely without interruption or criticism. This will have the dual benefit of quelling the overly vocal contributors and helping the less vocal to speak their minds freely. It is amazing to me how shy people will often rise to the occasion and deliver amazing input to a brainstorming session, provided they have been given the chance. I need to re-emphasize that when people contribute to the brainstorming session, care must be taken not to demean or criticize or else you are simply wasting yours and your team's time.

Pareto Analysis

Pareto analysis refers to the use of bar graphs to convey information that has been placed in order of its significance. Here is an example of a Pareto chart for top sales of widgets based on occurrence in U.S. States:

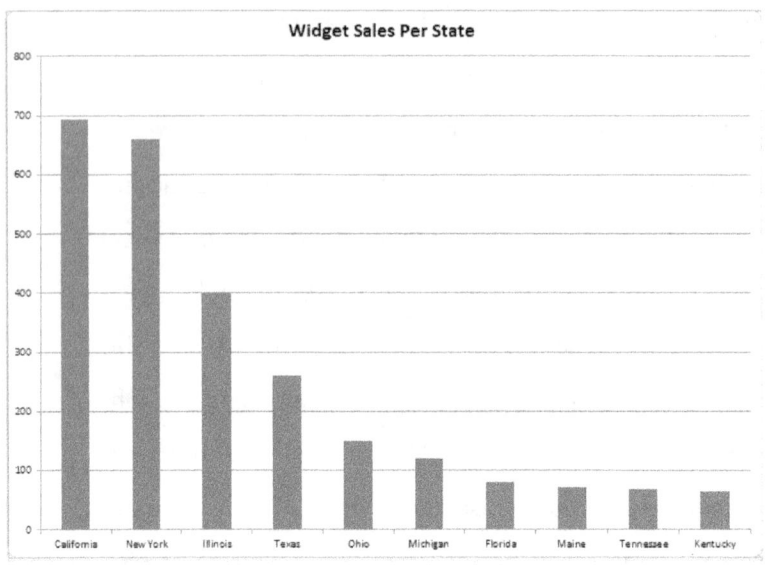

This Pareto shows who "butters your bread". From the chart, you can see that sales in California and New York account for much more than half of the entire sale – throw in Illinois and that accounts for almost 70%. To maximize revenues, you need to proportion your marketing expenditures accordingly.

Intuitive Decision Making

Unfortunately, in business not all decisions can be pared down to a quantitative solution. Remember, I'm an engineer, so how do you think that makes me feel! At some point, you are going to have to rely on good old fashioned intuition or "gut feel", it's almost unavoidable. To make matters worse, phrases like *"extinction by instinct"* have been coined to warn of the dangers of gut feel decision making. However, sometimes you simply will not have all of the variables available, so you will need to "feel" your way through. You can take heart in the fact that since it is a business that you built and therefore likely know every nut, bolt, sinew and nerve, you are *the* expert decision maker for your business. The following quote, from noted author Ray Bradbury gives us inspiration when faced with the need to make qualitative decisions:

'If we listened to our intellect we'd never have a love affair; we'd never have a friendship. We'd never go into business, because we'd be cynical: "It's gonna go wrong." or "She's going to hurt me." or "I've had a couple of bad love affairs, so therefore . . ."

Well, that's nonsense.

You're going to miss life.

You've got to jump off the cliff and build your wings on the way down.'

A brilliant analysis: "*...build your wings on the way down*". This statement nicely conveys the need to think very quickly *and* accurately. This idea was touched upon much earlier, although I must admit not nearly as eloquently, when I mentioned the abilities that would serve potential entrepreneurs well. Specifically; having the ability to insulate oneself from the inevitable unknowns and unknowables, having flexibility and nimbleness and I should add; maintaining an open mind and a sense of urgency. *Flexibility and nimbleness* are the characteristics that will allow you to build those wings very quickly and an open mind will tell you when you need to.

Some decisions, however, won't be as time constrained but may have to be made with very limited factual information. In this case, it is important to take as much time as you can; even "sleep on it" if you can before deciding. *Never let someone force you in to making a snap decision - yourself included!* Once you are ready, make the decision but, do not waiver. Do not act contrite. Be strong and confident in your analysis and your beliefs. That's strong leadership.

Net Present Value (NPV)

Learning about NPV calculations is our first foray into the realm of management accounting. This calculation is absolutely vital for deciding whether or not to invest in a capital project. Also, the method can easily be used to evaluate whether or not to start a business too; which is really just one huge, ongoing project made of many small ones.

Before we start, you need an understanding of a key concept in accounting and in economics, which is the concept of the *time value of money*. The time value of money basically stipulates that, a dollar is "worth more" or has greater purchasing power now than it will over time. This reduction in the value of a currency over time is the result of overall price increases; also known as inflation. So how can we compare future and present currency value on an "apples to apples" basis? We use the technique of *discounting* to calculate the buying power a currency in the future into today's currency value. This is known as the present value (PV) calculation. Let's use an example to clarify (you knew this was coming, didn't you?)

Find the present value (today's equivalent amount) of $100 in two years in the future assuming a discount rate of 2%

- **PV = FV (1+discount rate/100)^time**

Where;

Discount rate = a return that you could otherwise achieve if you invested elsewhere

PV = value of the currency today

FV = value of the currency in the future at future dollar value (not today's value!)

Time = years into the future

So,

PV = \$100 / (1 +0.02)^2

PV = \$96.11

Simply put, a \$100 dollar bill, 2 years from now is the same as about \$96 today. Therefore, if someone borrows \$96 from you today, "technically" they will need to pay you back \$100 in two years just to account for lost buying power eroded by inflation. This accounts for inflationary effects only; interest on top of that is another matter altogether.

So, we now have a mechanism to discount future cash flows back to today's dollars for exact comparison. Now suppose you are considering a project that will cost \$20,000 right now to get going. Suppose that you have calculated (conservatively!) that the following cash flows will result from this \$20,000 investment:

Project Cash Flows:

Start = ($20,000)

End of Year 1 = $500

End of Year 2 = $5000

End of Year 3 = $10000

End of Year 4 = $12000

End of Year 5 = $8000

The numbers look promising but, as we just proved using PV, the future cash flows are actually inflated if taken at par. For example, that $12,000 in year 4 is actually nothing like $12,000 once it has been calculated back into today's dollars (at a 3% discount rate) it is actually $10,662. As a matter of fact, many people would look at the above cash flows and assume that the 5 year net profit would be calculated as follows:

Net cash flow = -$20,000 + $500 +$5,000 + $10,000 +$12,000 + $8,000

= $15,500

And,

ROI = $15,500 / $20,000 x 100%

    = 77.5% right?

Well, sorry to say....WRONG! This is incorrect because it is actually overinflated. Let's investigate. To determine whether this investment is really worth considering, I will calculate and total the PV for each year (assuming a 3% discount rate = the return that you could otherwise achieve if you invested the $20,000 elsewhere) and add them up to calculate the NPV.

NPV = -$20,000 + $500/(1.03)^1 + $5,000/(1.03)^2 + $10,000/(1.03)^3 + $12,000/(1.03)^4 + $8,000/(1.03)^5

NPV = -$20,000 + $485 + $4,576 + $9,151 + $10,662 + $6,901

NPV = $11,775

ROI = $11775 / $20000 x 100% = 58.88%

So, for a $20,000 investment, over 5 years you will receive back the equivalent to $31,775 (minus the $20,000 = $11,775) expressed in today's dollars; a 59% rate of return. Anything above $0 is technically acceptable, but to be conservative you would want to see a good sized figure, well above $0. This project is therefore a good deal; especially since you were conservative in your cash flow projections.

Payback Period

The payback period is defined as the time that is required to recover the cost of an investment. The payback period is very similar to the NPV calculation, but is often not done using discounting methods. Personally, I think that is a huge mistake and will yield deceivingly short payback periods. To avoid this problem, I prefer to use *discounted* cash flow projections to estimate my payback periods. Here is the approach:

Let's re-use the above discounted cash flow projections for the project.

NPV = -$20,000 + $485 + $4,576 + $9,151 + $10,662 + $6,901

To calculate the payback period, all that we have to do is determine when the $20,000 capital cost gets repaid. I will list the years and the net return:

Net end of Year 1: -$20,000+$485 = -$19,515

Net end of Year 2: -$20,000+$485+$4,576 = -$14,939

Net end of Year 3: -$20,000+$485+$4,576+$9,151 = -$5,788

Net end of Year 4: -$20,000+$485+$4,576+$9,151+$10,662 = $4,834

So, as you can see, the net value of the project switches from a loss to a gain somewhere between year three and year four. You can actually interpolate the exact month if you want – I would actually estimate six or seven months into the fourth year the net goes from a negative number to zero. So, with this result, an investor would need to ask "can I wait three and a half years for my investment to be re-captured?"

The Eight Entrepreneurial Questions

For getting your processes set correctly from the beginning, I have saved the best for last. The *"eight entrepreneurial questions"* is one of the finest decision making tools that I know of for start-up focused decision making AND for deciding on new ventures within an established business. I learned it from Simon Barnes and Tim Meldrum, Professors of Entrepreneurship at the Imperial College Business School. Here is how the tool works. Suppose that you have identified a business idea, and you want to see if your idea can be considered something more than just an idea; a *market opportunity*. Here is an overview of how it works:

Eight Entrepreneurial Questions Model

Eight Entrepreneurial Questions Model Explained

1) Propose a Business Idea (using Lotus Blossom and weighted spreadsheet)

2) Answer first 4 test questions

3) If any questions are incorrect then make changes and start again

4) If all four questions are correct then Business Idea is now a Market Opportunity

5) Test Market Opportunity with next 4 questions

6) If any questions are incorrect then make changes and start back at Market Opportunity

7) If all four questions are correct then Market Opportunity is now a Business Opportunity

Let's take a closer look at the model by starting with the first four tests:

1) Is there a market for the business?

As I have mentioned numerous times in this book, does your business idea, if implemented correctly, solve a perceived problem in the market? If so, is there a significant enough market to support your idea? You need to show that there is.

2) Is there proof of the concept?

Do you have a prototype made or have you demonstrated the service? Can you display how it works? If you are going to be sourcing funding, these questions will be asked. You need to negotiate for capital from a position of strength, with all of your ducks in a row, which means having a working, tangible model for people to see. When I started my speaker company, I built several different prototypes to show to customers and to stereo shop owners for consignment deals. When I started my microbrewery, I made dozens of different beers for submission to the alcohol regulators for analysis; to bankers to address their curiosity; to investors who were considering investing in the business and to potential customers. We had a brand created and a label already designed, but sometimes words are not enough. You need something tangible.

3) Is the timing right?

Do you have a reasonable amount time to donate to the project - can you work on the business on a full time basis? Do you carry a full-time job with an employer and if so are you prepared to quit that job? Do you have significant family commitments? Is the public ready for your idea or is the timing premature? Has the need for your business idea moved on?

4) What is the potential size of the business; is it scalable and salable?

Your business is going to start out small; no doubt about it. This question pertains to the long-run perspective. If you can demonstrate how your business model is capable of earning royalties, signing up subscriptions, licensing out, being profitably expanded or being franchised, the answer is a resounding: "Yes! It is scalable and here is how….". Anything less than that means that you may just be creating a job for yourself. Not a legacy and not an investable value-creating venture, just a job. Again, think about your exit strategy and especially your investor's exit strategy. Most backers will have no interest in a business that lacks great potential and a clean and profitable exit.

OK, if you got by the first four questions, your business idea definitely has merit and has now been promoted to a *market opportunity* and you are away to the races! If, however, you got a "no" to any of the questions, you have pinpointed a problematic area and now have the option of altering your model and testing again. After you get past the first four questions, the next step is to test your market opportunity with four more questions, 5 to 8.

5) Can I marshal the resources to properly start-up and run the business?

Do you have the required money, do you have the necessary collateral to borrow the money or can you presell some ownership in the business to get money? Note: be very careful with preselling shares due to legal reasons and implications with securities laws – consult your lawyer first. Remember, cash is the lifeblood of the business, and you will need enough cash to set the business up, carry receivables, manage inventories, remit taxes, pay worker's compensation insurance and pay salaries *long before* you start to see significant cash flowing back into the business from your sales. Sounds bleak I know, and that is why I have emphasized conservatism in your financial analyses throughout the book. Many start-ups get going well enough, but falter not long after when they run short of cash. Sadly, if this happens to you, be aware that this likely marks the end of the road for your business as you know it. You will very likely either have to sell a much larger portion (probably control) of your *now proven* business or let it die, lose your paid-in capital and then have to honor any personal guarantees that you may have signed. Not a pretty scenario and totally avoidable if you are vigilant and plan well. Also, be aware of the legions of deep-pocketed opportunists out there just salivating to find a proven, distressed company for the pickings. These folks care *not* about the efforts that you have put into your business, because they are searching for a bargain. Be mindful of this. Make sure that you have access to much more money than the lowest of your conservatively projected **_accumulated_** negative cash flows. You will be really happy that you did when you arrive at greener pastures with 100% control of your company.

Entrepreneurial question five isn't just about marshaling the finances to run the business. There are many other resources that you must consider, such as, intellectual capital. Do you have the knowledge or does your team have the knowledge to make money in this market space? Do you have a list of potential customers? How much intimate knowledge have you on your competitors? Can you secure more capital if you miscalculated and end up stuck in the valley of death too long? All of the questions lead to the same conclusion: resources...can you get them?

6) Is this business for me?

Is this business your passion? Would you or have you ever been involved in this type of work as a hobby, volunteer or profession? Do you find the business so exciting that 14 hour days wouldn't bother you? Do you have either a natural inclination towards the business or many years of experience in it? Hopefully you do, because most investors need to see strong evidence of expert knowledge, commitment and experience before they fork over a penny. From personal experience, I can also tell you that mustering the energy to work extended hours week in, week out, will seem surprisingly effortless *provided you love the business.*

7) Can I build the best team for the venture?

This is critical. If the number one reason for new businesses failing is a lack of cash, assembling the wrong team is a very close second. If you can't rely on your team to get things done, to carry their share of the work, to be professional and trustworthy, then you are finished *before you even start*. You and your partners **all** need to be engaged, and you need to have equity share distributions set proportional to the amount of engagement and commitment that each of you will have. Get the right team, clearly define everyone's goals and objectives for each year, prepare a shot gun clause in the partnership agreement to keep everyone honest and hardworking and then you are covered either way. For partnerships, I recommend that the partners work together to hash out a tentative agreement and for each partner have his/her *own* lawyer vet the document. Sharing lawyers can cause really sticky problems later on. Been there, done that and I *don't* recommend it.

8) How will the business make money?

So, what is the business model? Put bluntly, how do you convert your efforts into cash? Make sure that you have a proven market and don't believe "if you build it, they will come" because if you are wrong, *you* will pay dearly. That mindset should stay in the movies.

So those are the eight entrepreneurial questions. If you got through all of them, your business idea has officially become *business opportunity* and you are well on your way to establishing your new product/service.

Now, guess what? YOU HAVE FINISHED THE PRIMERS!! Quite a bit of information wasn't it? So, think back to the discussion at the beginning; about the myth that to be an entrepreneur you need to be born with certain inherent characteristics. *Do you now see why this has been confirmed to be a myth and that entrepreneurship is indeed a learned process?* With your new perspective on marketing, accounting, economics, strategy, process improvement and decision making, you should have a very different view than before you studied this section. Congratulations on work well done. Let's move on to stories from the trenches.

Chapter 5 - Stories from the Trenches

It is not the critic who counts; not the man who points out how the strong man stumbles, or where the doer of deeds could have done them better. The credit belongs to the man who is actually in the arena, whose face is marred by dust and sweat and blood; who strives valiantly; who errs, who comes short again and again, because there is no effort without error and shortcoming; but who does actually strive to do the deeds; who knows great enthusiasms, the great devotions; who spends himself in a worthy cause; who at the best knows in the end the triumph of high achievement, and who at the worst, if he fails, at least fails while daring greatly, so that his place shall never be with those cold and timid souls who neither know victory nor defeat.

Theodore Roosevelt, 1910

Ok, so with a reasonable grounding in business concepts, let's turn our focus to some real world aspects and anecdotes of entrepreneurship. These stories come from my personal experiences and hard won lessons while running businesses. I believe that you will find these stories very helpful at some point in your venture. These anecdotes focus on things that went very right and things that went very wrong while I was pursuing my dreams. I would remind you as outlined in the Introduction; my job is to help you to avoid stepping into bear traps. Read carefully and learn.

Research

Probably the most important and hard-won lesson I learned when starting a business, was to "always take the path of least resistance" when performing literally thousands of tasks during the start-up and scale-up phases. "Well, we all know *that!*" did I hear you say? Well, from my experience, everyone knows this, but very few follow through. Stepping off the path of least resistance can be insidious. This is especially so when you are bogged way down in the trenches during the start-up phase of your venture; ESPECIALLY if you are trying too hard to bootstrap your way through. In hindsight, I wish that I could get all of the time and dollars back that I frittered away before I learned this lesson, because both were *significant*. So, how do you ensure that you remain on the path of least resistance? To get your venture started, you will surely need to compile staggering amounts of vital information in a very short timeframe. With regard to getting information, the first thing that you must realize is that there are virtually unlimited sources of information out there. Be prepared to spend considerable time processing information and doing so as thoroughly as possible. Once you have collected and consolidated sufficient, relevant information, you will then need to make sense of that information through the process of paring down, organizing and categorizing - separating the "wheat from the chaff". A daunting task, even if all goes perfectly. My opinion? *TOTALLY avoid this approach!* It is slow, inefficient, laborious, tedious, and it sucks the enthusiasm right out of you.

I believe that the key is to fast-track the research process; to get on and stay on *the path*. The ultimate fast-track to accurate, timely and critical information is to simply *have conversations with as many people relevant to your business as you can*. Sounds anticlimactic? Your competition will probably think so too! You shouldn't though because this is opposite to migrating away from the path of least resistance - actually it will situate you at the *dead center* of the path. Here is the beauty of this approach. If you chat with the right people, ask the right questions and listen very carefully, you will reap *volumes* of priceless information in just a brief chat. Build your network by speaking to everyone that you can. Join entrepreneurship clubs. Go to conventions. Use social networking to meet people. Believe it or not, you can even go speak to your future competitors – ethically though, otherwise you are simply spying. You would be amazed at the amount of information that they are willing to offer. Of course, for every question that you ask of them, expect at least one back. Exercise extreme discretion when answering; being ethical is a must, but tipping your hand is foolish. Done correctly, speaking to a future competitor can be incredibly helpful. I actually hired one of my prospective competitors to help me with some financial projections during due diligence. His projections ended up being almost dead on! So, don't be shy and don't concern yourself with fears about the competitor stealing your ideas, because above all, you're going to be very discreet about what you disclose. It is also important for you to realize that unless you appear to your future competitor as resource-rich as Sir Richard Branson, I can assure you that they won't think twice about you five minutes after you leave - because they are likely way too busy in the trenches themselves. Right from the due diligence stage, commit *on paper* to meet a certain number of people each day, week and month and then just do it. Learn, learn and learn some more, but never set out to reinvent the wheel. One last thing, if you have a formal grand opening, consider extending an invitation to the people that were particularly helpful to you.

Negotiating

So, what were the major challenges that I had to deal with when I began to build companies? TONS! Every day provided shockingly humbling experiences as I got to learn *from the trenches*, what to do and what *not* to do and why. For example, when I was working with the bank to secure a loan **_I didn't negotiate_** the interest rate on the small business loan! That's right; the *government-backed-essentially-risk-free-for-the-bank* small business loan. Rookie mistake! I should have realized that the bank undertook no risk whatsoever of default on this loan and, therefore, could have reduced the rate of interest. I didn't ask, so I didn't receive. Always ask; you may be quite pleased with the results.

When setting terms and prices with your suppliers; ask for the moon. You have NOTHING to lose by doing this and much to gain if you are successful. Emphasize your history or expert knowledge of the business to gain their confidence and to believe in your long-term success. Effectively, what you are trying to do is to make a de facto partner of them.

When I was starting out, my bottle supplier insisted on cash before release of materials. So, I made a point of *personally* delivering a certified cheque one week *before* I needed my bottles. The supplier had never seen such.....*enthusiasm* for paying bills before and it wasn't very long after that they voluntarily offered 30 day payment terms. I assure you, this wasn't the case with my competitors!

Managing cash

A fundamental mistake that I made was building a plant before building the brand. You might find this statement surprising but: *brands are value, plants are not*. Having been through the wringer more than once, I now see production plants as a mass of costly, failure-prone, hard to maintain, depreciating assets. For tax reasons, that can be a good thing, depending on how mature your business is, but generally speaking, a plant is an expensive thing to carry; especially during the start-up phase. In hindsight, I should have saved our precious cash for marketing and advertising and hiring the best salespeople that I could get. Just like the conclusions in the winery case study, I should have had product manufacturing contracted out. In all honesty, building and running the plant was a painful experience. There was very little equipment reliability which kept me behind the eight ball constantly with lagging inventory levels. If you are considering a manufacturing-based business, do yourself a big favor and explore contracting out first. Once your brand is established, you can build a reliable dream plant – but later; when it actually *saves* you money to do so. Beyond making monetary sense, this is a much less risky approach to establishing your brand, since you don't need to outlay the capital for an underutilized plant.

Time Management

Another mistake that I made, and this is also connected to the manufacturing plant, was not having the time to go to meet with customers every single day. As a matter of fact, since I was tied up running the plant, I had very little time for sales and promotion at all. This was a significant lost opportunity because customers would really have appreciated the president of the company taking the time to come to speak with them and listen to their concerns and suggestions. So, my advice; think twice about structuring your business in a way such that you wind up being tasked with menial jobs that yield a comparatively small return on your time. In my case, brewing beer garnered tens of dollars in revenue for each dollar that I was paid, but spending time with our customers and end-users would have yielded hundreds of dollars for every dollar that I was paid; simple economics.

Another thing that, in hindsight, I would do differently if I were to start another manufacturing business would be to have a much more stringent quality control system in place. This would have saved hundreds of thousands of dollars by avoiding recalls and avoiding the loss of customers who purchased sub-par product. While I am generally a proponent of finding creative ways to save money, bootstrapping any quality control system will come back to haunt you; I guarantee it.

Bootstrapping

The bootstrapping that was done allowed the plant to be built at a fraction of the price, perhaps one tenth the cost of a brand new showpiece plant. We purchased used large fermenters for $5,000 each instead of $50,000. We purchased a used bottling line for around $100,000 however this would have been over $1,000,000 had we gone to the original equipment manufacturer and bought new.   Using this methodology allowed us to afford the assets required to make the business successful. If we had to commit to brand new equipment instead, then gathering the monies to pay for the equipment while retaining a decent level of ownership would have been a significant challenge. One word of warning, if you do go the used equipment route; you must either be very good at maintenance or you should have sufficient funds to hire a good mechanic and electrician.   Being plagued with constant equipment failures will put you out of business.

Brewhouse area of our microbrewery

In the picture above, the tanks, heat exchangers, pumps, piping, wiring and engineering would have cost somewhere in the order of $200,000 - $250,000 to purchase and install. I managed it for about a fifth of that when I learned to TIG weld, sourced quality used tanks and did much of the installation myself. These were hugely value-added activities that I was undertaking, which is what bootstrapping is all about. Replacing welders, plumbers, engineers and equipment manufactures is money in the bank.

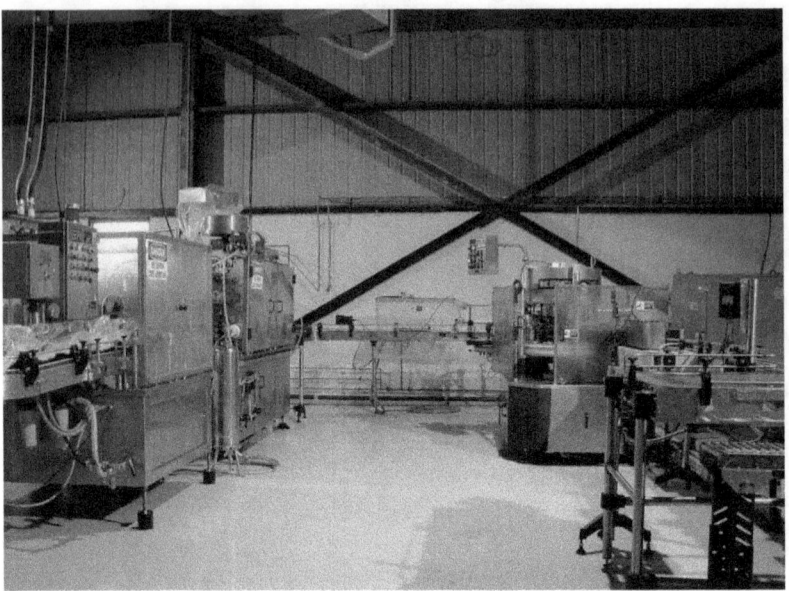

Aseptic 24 Valve Rotary Filling Line

The used filling line shown above was purchased for a fraction of the price that it cost the original owner. If you decide to go this route with very complex equipment, do yourself a big favor and contract a person that understands the equipment to accompany you and advise you before you purchase. We chose to do that and never regretted the cost.

Unknowns and Unknowables

When I was running the company, I was always amazed at the way curve balls would seemingly come out of nowhere. One Sunday afternoon, I was relaxing in the backyard with my wife and newborn daughter when I received a call from our security company. Apparently, someone really wanted our cash register, so they put a rock through the front window to get it. When I arrived at the brewery, I saw that the "perp" (I always wanted to use that word!) did not make a clean entrance through the broken window - as indicated by the trail of blood to and from the spot where the register once sat. Too bad for this guy that the register was empty….HA! So, what was the lesson that I learned that day? Always keep my valuable assets out of direct sight of the window; way too much temptation for local felons.

Work/Life Balance

Another not so fond memory that I have was being at the hospital when my daughter was being born and having to take calls from the brewery *while we were in the birthing room!!* The nurses couldn't believe it; they suggested that I get a new job. The same kind of thing happened when my wife and I were on our honeymoon in Hawaii; call after call about issues at the brewery. Neither of these are my wife's favorite stories *I assure you!* Needless to say, she is a most patient woman. When you become an entrepreneur, be prepared to give up a huge amount of autonomy. What you should glean from this is that your business will become a pseudo appendage. If you have, or are expecting a child, think very carefully about the timing of your start up. While I understand completely that you want to provide a legacy for your family, you don't want the trials and tribulations of a start-up interfering with the happiness of your family life – especially when your children are very young.....or being born. Compromises are possible though. When I was about nine years old my parents started a printing company. Rather than letting the obligations of the business interfere with the family, my parents involved my sisters and I in the business. On weekends, we would go to the unit where the business was, and we would help out. It was enjoyable for us as a family; and no doubt it played a key role in my fascination with entrepreneurship.

Think "SUCCESS!"

Now, here is an interesting one. In the beginning stages of the company, I would keep our finished goods inventories very low in order to maintain cash levels. From an order fulfillment perspective, I felt that this was a good practice since I was not actually *expecting* anything but slow, steady growth. Well, wasn't I surprised when at 5:00 PM on a Friday a new customer phoned, out of the blue, and ordered all the beer that I had in inventory? So, on the heels of my twelve hour day, I had to prep to brew immediately, which meant I was staying for another 15 hours. I stayed all night and wrapped up the next morning; 27 hours in total. Now, had I *truly* believed in success, I would have worried a less about my cash balance and more about my ability to meet product demand. That day (and night and day) I learned, the hard way, that product demand for new companies can be extremely volatile; increasing/decreasing in massive spikes, not in a predictable linear fashion. For me, this was one of those "unknowns" that I mention throughout the book. My advice? During the embryonic stages of your company, even though holding extra inventory will stress your cash position somewhat, you would be wise not to risk lost revenues by being too frugal and not having the goods to deliver if someone wants them. Once your company has matured, demand will become much more predictable and at this point that you can really manage your inventories well; with a razor's edge precision. The only exception to this scenario is for businesses that have the ability to accommodate virtually any level of demand, such as electronic information (e-books, music and software). So, the moral of the story? When you start your business, plan for success. I know; it sounds obvious but what I mean by this is that you must set yourself up for winning every single day.

More Curve Balls

One of the things that I certainly did not incorporate into my business plan was how often the delivery truck was going to get stolen. I probably should have added a provision in my pro forma income statements for *amortized grand theft auto charges*! At one point, they were stealing our truck at least once per week - and the police were legitimately WAY too busy with bigger things than to stake out our place. These morons even stole the truck that we rented to replace the truck that was stolen! It eventually got so ridiculous that I asked our driver to start wrapping the front wheel and frame of the truck with a massive chain and lock every night. Not long after that, I arrived to see our hot-wired truck sitting in the parking lot, still running, with the driver's door wide open and a ten foot long single skid mark on the pavement that occurred when the thief attempted to drive the truck with the chain-locked wheel. Better.....but still not perfect. So, the next thing I did was to ask the driver to pull out the starter relays from under the hood every night. This prevented the truck from starting and eventually ended the crime spree. Keeping a sense of humor about it, I seriously considered producing a beer called *Stolen-Truck Lager!* I decided not to go ahead with it because I believed that the only people that it would appeal to and would want to buy it would be the guys that were stealing my truck every night – and clearly they were *way* too busy to drink beer. Besides, they would steal the beer, not buy it!

One of my not so fond memories of the brewery days was the ongoing bad relations with our next door neighbor. We were situated in an industrial unit and unfortunately the neighbor (and their 50 employees) didn't appreciate the smell of beer being made. The property management director was called to our unit almost every day. It got really messy. I managed to engineer a reasonable solution when I installed a massive exhaust fan that kept our unit in a constant low pressure condition. This stopped the migration of odors to the neighbors unit and ended the complaints.

Another interesting day at work was when the entire eastern part of the United States and Canada lost power for a full day. I was in the middle of boiling a batch of beer when everything stopped. Honestly, it was the eeriest silence that I have ever heard in my life. I remember everyone standing around their cars listening to the news of what had happened. Amazingly I only lost one batch of beer from this.

All of these anecdotes fall under the category of "things that just happen". People have no control over such oddities. So when you prepare your business plan, focus on the things that you really can control. Cash levels, inventory levels, customer satisfaction, having good rapport with your bank, accountant and lawyer. These things lie at the heart of your value proposition. The things that just happen are going to happen no matter what you do.

In the planning process of your business, try to do your research in a reasonable amount of time and then get going. Don't take two plus years planning the business as I did; momentum is lost if you do. Make your business plan reasonably concise and as fact-based as possible and then move onto financing and start-up quickly. Use the tools that I have shown you. I didn't have them when I was starting and really would have benefited if I had.

Final Thoughts

Well, it's been 24 months since I started this book and I must say that my intentions in the beginning were much less ambitious. Originally, I only planned to write an article on profit maximization....then I thought, *why not a white paper instead*....or *perhaps a blog*......or *maybe a how-to manual* and in the end; this book. Seems that I had more to say than I originally intended! Process improvement specialists call this "scope creep" however I prefer to call it....*thinking big*.

So, now that you have reached the end, has your confidence increased? Do you feel more empowered to start your own venture or launch a new product or service in your current business? Do you have a better understanding of key issues such as liability, risk mitigation, project analysis, decision making, accounting, leadership and general management? What about the effects that starting a business will have on relationships, such as family and friends? Do you understand now that the value of your idea is directly proportional to how *few* people can do the same thing (think professional athlete as a good example)? Do you understand that without well thought out, *efficient* processes, you *cannot* maximize the profit potential of your organization?

I encourage you to use the tools discussed in this book to help you find and analyze opportunities and ensure that your processes are indeed functioning at the most efficient level. Using tools such as the Lotus Blossom Diagram, weighted spreadsheet and NPV will allow you to create, rank and analyze your ideas. Strategic tools such as PERT, SWOT and Porter's Five Forces will help to structure the approach to analyzing the business environment. Understanding the possible ramifications of a price increase will allow you to prepare for all scenarios in advance; knowledge is power. Being able to look your banker in the eye and tell him that you created the pro forma financial reports and financial ratios and you based them on conservative cash flow analyses extending from detailed market research will be one of the most empowering things that you will do in you entrepreneurial career. This kind of approach will get you your loan. And you will deserve it.

Due to the relative brevity of this book, most topics were addressed from the "50,000 foot level" so there is much more to learn if you choose to. If any of the topics that we looked at really caught your imagination, then I strongly encourage you to delve in and learn all that you can about them. What I set out to do, once I finally admitted to myself that I was going to write a book, was to give would-be entrepreneurs and managers the tools that can be leveraged to help decide on a process path or business, investigate it, structure it, build it and then exit it (if you so choose). As I peruse the chapters, I strongly believe that this book is a complete document and one that should serve you well; provided that you are prepared to invest the time. I know that a book like this was nowhere to be found when I was starting out, and that's what I wanted to change.

Seize the Day

Aim for success the first time. As mentioned in the beginning, I do not want to prepare you to go from failure to failure. To do that you must avoid thought patterns like:

- "If I'm not successful in my business, I'll just start another one"

- "if my marriage fails, I'll get it right the second time"

- "If I select a bad business partner, I'll just get rid of her and find a better one"

Well, all that I can say is (in my opinion): wrong, wrong and WRONG! What if there are no second chances? It's probably unwise to ever assume that there will be. I suggest that when you undertake any project, either fully commit to the task or don't commit at all. I have a very good friend who laments, "I should have done *this* and should have tried *that* and if I had, my business would have survived for sure". Well, that might be true, and conversely, it might not.

I believe that one should do his/her best to stack the deck in one's favor to help increase the odds of success and reduce the odds of failure and feeling regret later. Having read this book will go a long way to accomplishing all of that. Looking at it positively, regret is a bit of a double-edged sword. Not wanting to feel regret can be a powerful catalyst for avoiding it; and that can push you to do all the right things. On the other hand, it can be a huge energy waster that lures you into complacency. Again I ask, what happens if there is no next time, if there is no opportunity for a second chance? For the vast majority of business start-up failures, it can be argued that the door to failure is wedged wide open as a result of a job NOT well done. I contend that if you fully commit to your project, make the very best decisions that you can, using appropriate professional input when needed, tenacity and focus, you will maximize your chances of success. If, however, you follow these steps and in the end still aren't successful, then there can never be regret. You can't *reasonably* look back and beat yourself up with thoughts like, "what if I had done this instead of that" if you optimized your decisions based on thoughtful and thorough analysis of the facts that were available. Hindsight in this case is about as valid as comparing your losing lottery ticket to the winning numbers and erroneously thinking: "I could have picked those numbers easily!", the glaring difference being that the lottery is a blind gamble, the business start-up is a process of optimizing decision making and mitigating risk.

So, when you pursue your dream business, do it with your eyes wide open. Be an *entrepreneur* never a maverick. Do your best so that you won't have to deal with that little voice in your head telling you that you *could have*, or you *should have* after it's too late. Doing your best takes the destructive power and the volume away from that little voice.

So, the time has come for me to thank you kindly for making the investment in my book. I wish you the greatest success - notice I didn't say luck - in your venture, and I hope that what you have learned here will play at least a small part in that success. Now, go seize the day.

The Author

Cameron Howe resides just outside of Toronto, Canada and has three passions in life; his family (hidden behind the camera!), piano and getting into the trenches to help businesses increase profits by streamlining their processes. Cameron is President and CEO of *Howe-2-Profit (H2P)*, a management consulting firm dedicated to help people manage their business processes more profitably. *Cameron* can be reached at info@howe2profit.com.